Images of
Royal
Derby

Royal visits to the Derby area seen through
the eyes of the Evening Telegraph

Images of Royal Derby

Royal visits to the Derby area seen through
the eyes of the Evening Telegraph

Breedon Books
Publishing Company
Derby

First published in Great Britain by
The Breedon Books Publishing Company Limited
Breedon House, 44 Friar Gate, Derby, DE1 1DA.
1998

**All the photographs in this book can be ordered as black and
white prints. The visits of the 1990s in Chapter Eight are available
in colour. Telephone the Derby Evening Telegraph Photographic
Department on 01332 291111 Ext 3803 for more details.**

ISBN 1 85983 144 3

Printed and bound by Butler & Tanner Ltd., Selwood Printing Works,
Caxton Road, Frome, Somerset.

Colour separations by Freelance Repro, Leicester.

Jackets printed by Lawrence-Allen, Avon.

Contents

Foreword

ROYAL visits to Derby – as recorded in the pages of the *Derby Evening Telegraph* throughout the 20th century – have always been an occasion for public rejoicing.

But it was a different story throughout the Middle Ages when Kings were frequent visitors to Derby as they passed through on State affairs or came to hunt in Duffield forest.

They often brought with them a large retinue of arrogant followers who lived well at the expense of the local people.

King John stayed in Derby in 1200 and again four years later.

In 1263, Henry III and his son Prince Edward were busy laying waste to the lands of the rebellious Earl Robert de Ferrers.

By 1291 it was the turn of Edward I who was welcomed by the Abbot and Canons of Darley Abbey.

Edward II called at Derby in 1323 and 1325 to hunt in Duffield forest, and Henry IV was here before the Battle of Shrewsbury.

Mary Queen of Scots was not a willing guest during her years of captivity and Charles I spent a night while he was negotiating a treaty with the Scottish.

He also marched through Derby from Nottingham where he had raised his army during the Civil War.

The Duke of York – later King George VI – during his visit to Ley's Malleable Castings in 1933.

The Duke of Kent's tour of Derby factories in 1941.

The Princess Royal is greeted by Sir Ian Walker, Lord Lieutenant of Derbyshire, on arrival at Derby's Midland Station in November 1951.

Excited youngsters wait for the Queen on her 1957 visit to Derby.

Bonnie Prince Charlie was an unwelcome visitor when he invaded with his Scottish troops in 1745, although a statue of him now stands near the Cathedral.

By Victorian times, the happier nature of Royal visits as we know them was becoming established.

In 1832, Princess Victoria – as she then was – and the Duchess of Kent passed through Derby on the way to Chatsworth. Later, as Queen, she returned with her husband in 1842.

In 1849, the Queen and Prince Albert came to Derby by train and stayed at the newly-opened Midland Hotel.

Victoria's son, the Prince of Wales – later Edward VII – named two wards in the Nightingale wing of the old infirmary and presented prizes at Derby School Speech Day in 1872.

Lavish decorations around Derby marked

the Prince's return in 1881 to visit the Royal Show which was being held in the town. But even they were outdone by the show put on ten years later.

Queen Victoria was so delighted by her visit to Derby on May 21, 1891 that she knighted the Mayor, Alfred Haslam. During this trip she laid the foundation stone for the Derbyshire Royal Infirmary. After her death, King Edward VII visited in 1906 when the Royal Show was in town again. He also paused at the Spot to unveil the famous statue of his late mother.

Many Royal family members pulled in a visit to Derby while they were staying at Chatsworth House – including Queen Mary who visited the infirmary on December 10, 1913.

King George V made his first visit to Derby on June 29, 1921, for the Royal Show and after the excesses of the visits at the end of the 19th century he specifically asked that no money

The Queen Mother arrives at Derby Council House in June 1971.

should be spent by the Corporation on street decorations. Apart from decoration of the station at the railway company's expense his wish was granted.

The Prince of Wales – later King Edward VIII before his abdication – visited Derby in February 1928 after calling at Ashbourne to "turn up" the ball to start the annual Shrovetide football game.

When he came again in June 1932, he insisted that details of his visit were withheld until the last minute to enable him to see life under 'normal conditions'. He visited the Rural Community Council Offices, Derby Unemployed Men's Club and TocH headquarters.

Markeaton and Darley parks were opened on June 30, 1931 by the Duke of Kent who visited Rolls-Royce on the same day.

On May 3, 1933, the Duke of York – later King George VI – visited Ley's Malleable Castings.

Another Royal Show in Derby the same year drew back King George and Queen Mary.

The Derbyshire Royal Infirmary was the destination of the Duchess of Gloucester in

Princess Diana on her 1985 visit to Derby.

Prince Charles meets Mrs Fanny Berry at Warwick House Old People's Home in Bonsall Avenue, Littleover, a week before her 109th birthday.

The Queen meets young loyal fans in 1992.

1936 where she opened a £90,000 extension.

While Derby suffered like the rest of Britain during World War Two, morale received a massive boost when the new King, George VI, and his Queen visited in 1940.

The Princess Royal was another visitor during the war years along with the Duke and Duchess of Kent and the Duke and Duchess of Gloucester.

Derby met a young Princess Elizabeth in 1949 when she officially opened the Council House. Her next visit was as Queen in 1957.

In the 1960s, several visits from the Duke of Edinburgh gave him a chance to speak out for local industries like aero engine building and the railways.

A rich crop of Royal guests throughout the 1970s brightened up Derby, but the crowning glory was the day in 1977 when the Queen officially made the town into a city.

Derby had its first look at Diana, Princess of Wales, in the 1980s, with two more visits in the 1990s.

The final decade of the century also saw two major visits from the Queen, in 1992 and 1997.

In this book we hope to bring you a flavour – in words and pictures – of many of the Royal visits to Derby in the 20th century and how they were seen by the city's evening newspaper.

Chapter One

Derby Lives a Fairytale

"THE OLD borough of Derby lived today a story which might have been lifted straight out of a book of fairy tales, when beneath a canopy of blue skies, amid a blaze of colour, and with stately pageantry and splendour, the King and Queen paid their official visit to the Royal Show at Osmaston".

With the above words the *Derby Evening Telegraph* began its Royal Visit Souvenir edition of Wednesday July 5, 1933.

A look back at newspaper reports of Royal visits in the years before World War Two offers a rewarding glimpse of a prosaic style of writing which is long gone.

The 1933 visit was the fifth time the Royal Show had been held in Derby. The first time was in 1839 when Osmaston Park – setting for all Derby's Royal Shows – was still the home of the Wilmot Horton family.

It is not clear whether any Royalty came on that occasion.

When the show returned to Derby in 1881, the Prince of Wales – the future Edward VII – was happily doing such duties for his mother, Queen Victoria.

The Mayor of Derby, Alderman Abraham Woodiwiss, a railway millionaire, laid on sumptuous hospitality for him – even, it is said, having a private siding made for the Royal train. It cost him a lot, but he came out of it as Sir Abraham and Mayor for a second term.

Royal Show number three was in June 1906, and back came Edward as King. On his way from a reception in the Market Place to the showground he stopped at the Spot to unveil a statue of his late mother, presented to the town by Sir Alfred Haslam – Mayor at the time of the Queen's 1891 visit.

The fourth Derby Royal Show brought George V to the town in June 1921. He drove straight to the showground from the station and straight back four hours later. But the show recorded a record attendance of 125,000 over the five days.

Reporting of the event in the *Telegraph* made much of the "never-ending procession" of cars and other motor vehicles which poured through Derby's streets.

"Such a variety of cars has certainly never been seen in our midst. It took them, as we have said, four hours to pass on their way", wrote the *Telegraph*.

Despite a cooling breeze, ambulance men were called on to deal with two or three cases of fainting as crowds gathered at the railway station.

Heat was also intense on the "fairy tale" 1933 visit. Three hens and several pigs died at the showground as temperatures soared into the 80s.

But it did not prevent crowds 20 and 30 deep from lining the route of the carriage containing the King and Queen as they drove to the showground, which stood where Ascot Drive Industrial Estate later sprouted. Many onlookers donned bathing costumes, the *Telegraph* observed, but the Queen maintained her cool in a powder blue gown and matching sunshade. The King's suit and top hat were silver grey.

The century of Royal reporting had begun sombrely in 1901 with the death of Queen Victoria at 6.30pm on Tuesday January 22 at the age of 81. The *Derby Evening Telegraph* carried a brief announcement in its special 7.30pm edition that night with a full account next day.

The following year plans were well in hand in Derby to celebrate the Coronation of King Edward VII and Queen Alexandra when – with two days to go – the Coronation was postponed because the King had appendicitis. Street parties went ahead but the city bonfire and fireworks were postponed until the King had recovered in August.

In 1928 "Supreme joy reigned in Ashbourne", according to the *Telegraph*, when the Prince of Wales gave Royal patronage to Shrovetide football for the first time.

After "turning up" the ball on Shaw Croft, the Prince travelled to Derby in a Rolls-Royce car.

Some 230 children from the Railway Servants' Orphanage were out on the lawn to watch him drive by – but sadly they were too far from the road to see or be seen.

There was a complete absence of formality for the visit – in keeping with the Prince's wishes. On reaching the Market Place, and being received by the Mayor of Derby, Councillor A. Sturgess, the Prince turned to the hundreds of ex-servicemen and spent 20 minutes talking to them – delaying his official lunch.

Derby streets were lavishly decorated for the 1881 visit of the Prince of Wales – the future King Edward VII.

The *Telegraph* reported that "flappers", fashionably dressed women of the 1920s, "whispered ecstatically, 'Isn't he lovely?' as they clicked their cameras."

"He had a boyish habit of rubbing the right side of his bronzed face with two fingers when he was not shaking hands," the report continued.

The Prince went on to Rolls-Royce, then through Osmaston Park to Normanton and Pear Tree British Legion and the LMS carriage and wagon and locomotive works.

On May 2, 1933 the Duke of York, as President of the Industrial Welfare Society, began a two-day tour of factories in Derbyshire and Nottinghamshire.

He visited Stanton Ironworks and Lea Mills on the first day and Ley's Malleable Castings on May 3.

The *Telegraph* brought out a special edition on Monday May 6, 1935, to celebrate the Silver Jubilee of King George and Queen Mary.

At the end of that year, the Duke of Kent – "Ambassador of the Workless" – made a three-day visit to Derbyshire to tour unemployed occupational centres.

On December 17 he visited Belper and received a baby chair made in oak for his young son. The following day, in Derby, three-year-old Ann Hibberd of 73 Canal Street presented the Duke with a Royal Crown Derby china plaque as another present for the baby Prince.

During his visit he opened Community House, Kedleston Road, the new headquarters of the Derbyshire Rural Community Council before leaving for lunch at Kedleston Hall.

King George V died at five minutes to midnight on Monday, January 20, 1936. It was announced officially 20 minutes later and the *Telegraph* rushed out an early morning edition followed by a second special edition looking back on his life including his Derby visits.

In October there was more cheerful news to report as the Duchess of Gloucester paid her first official visit to Derby to lay the foundation stone of the new £90,000 extension at the Derbyshire Royal Infirmary.

She wore a violet woollen two-piece with lilac trim and a pointed velvet cap in a darker shade with a quill feather.

The year ended with the abdication crisis. Rumours of the relationship between the eligible Prince of Wales – who became King Edward VIII when his father died at the start of the year – and American divorcee Wallis Simpson had been circulating in American newspapers for more than a year. But the first mention in British newspapers came from Dr Alfred Blunt, Bishop of Bradford and former vicar of St Werburgh's, Derby, who told his diocesan conference that he hoped the King was aware of his need for the grace of God and would give "more positive signs of such awareness".

The King's abdication was announced in a late final edition of the *Derby Telegraph* on Thursday December 10, 1936 and the Duke of York was announced as the new King.

So, 1936 ended up as the year of three Kings and Derby was the scene of much celebration for the Coronation of King George VI and Queen Elizabeth in 1937.

St Peter's Street, Derby, decorated for Queen Victoria's Diamond Jubilee in 1897.

A postcard commemorating Edward VII's visit to the Royal Show in 1906.

King George V, at the Royal Show in June 1921, chats to a policeman.

The Prince of Wales leaves after opening the new ex-servicemen's headquarters in Normanton in 1928.

The Prince of Wales spent so long talking to ex-servicemen in Derby Market Place, that he was late for his official lunch, February 1928.

Final stop on the Prince's 1928 visit was the LMS Carriage and Wagon Works.

At Rolls-Royce, the Prince was accompanied by the Mayor of Derby, Councillor Sturgess.

The Duke of York on his visit to Ley's Malleable Castings in May 1933.

A dignified look straight into the *Telegraph* photographer's lens from the Duke of York – later to become King George VI – on his 1933 visit.

Crowds of well-wishers welcomed King George V and Queen Mary to the Royal Show in July 1933.

King George V acknowledges the cheering crowds by lifting his silver grey top hat while Queen Mary shelters from the heat under a powder blue sunshade.

Major Walter Elliott, Minister of Agriculture, fed information to the King and Queen as they toured the Osmaston Showground – which later became Ascot Drive Industrial Estate.

Derby firm Joseph Mason was honoured to receive the Royal visitors at the 1933 show.

In 1936 the Duchess of Gloucester visited Derby to lay the foundation stone of new extensions to the Derbyshire Royal Infirmary. Here, the Duchess tours a guard of honour of nurses accompanied by the matron, Miss Ellen Kenyon and Lady Inglefield, President of the Infirmary.

Decorations for the Coronation of King George VI and Queen Elizabeth in Derby's Market Place.

People of Derby queue to see the wreath being sent on behalf of the town to the funeral of King George V, January 1936.

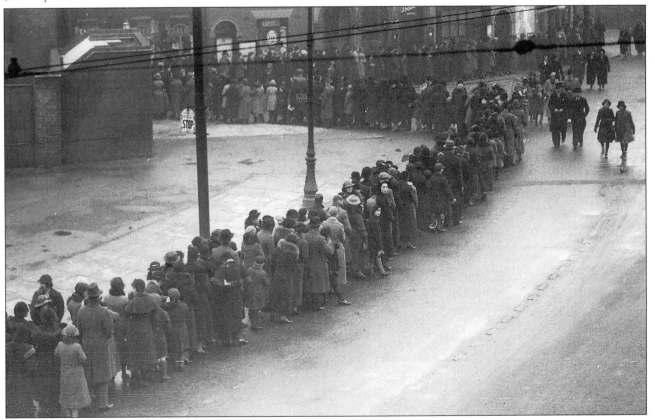

Ranby's famous store, which later made way for Debenhams, had the flags out for the 1937 Coronation of King George VI and Queen Elizabeth.

Lavish Coronation decorations in Derby's Market Hall.

A huge civic celebration in the Market Place marked the 1937 Coronation.

One of many Coronation street parties held in Derby.

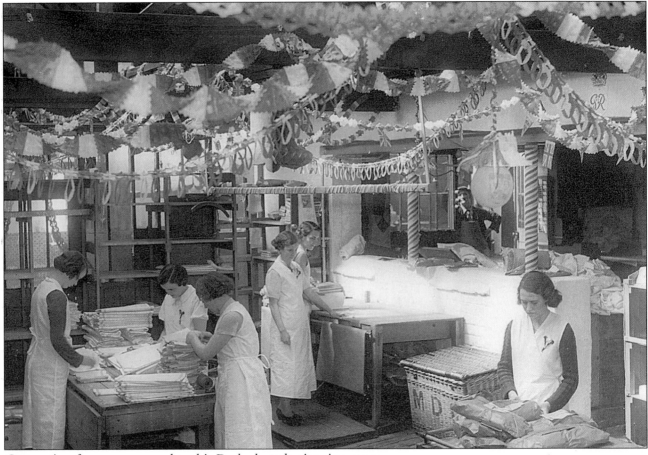

Coronation fever even spread to this Derby laundry ironing room.

Eagle Street, Derby, had the flags out too in patriotic style.

Chapter Two

The War Years

IN THE middle of the Battle of Britain, when Rolls-Royce in Derby was working all-out supplying the RAF with Merlin aero-engines, King George VI and Queen Elizabeth made a morale-boosting visit to the factory.

It was a closely-guarded secret until the last minute. Even when the *Telegraph* reported it, the newspaper was forbidden by censors from saying which Derby factory the Royal couple toured.

The chief reason given for the visit was so that the King could meet and inspect some Indian troops in an unidentified south-west Derbyshire village – which was, in fact, Osmaston, near Ashbourne.

The King and Queen were met at the railway station on August 8, 1940, by the Mayor of Derby, Alderman Arthur Neal, and the King asked about the air raids on Derby.

Then the Royal party was driven to Osmaston, where the King was ceremonially offered Silver coins. Later, their Majesties visited the cookhouse and the Queen was given some chapatis to take back to the Princesses Elizabeth and Margaret.

The *Telegraph* reported: "Her Majesty, like Queen Mary, never makes the mistake of dressing in drab colours. However dull or rainy the day, she is always dressed in becoming pastel shades."

On this day she wore a pale blue crepe dress with a long coat to match and grey suede shoes. Her halo hat was the same shade of duck-egg blue and she wore a double string of pearls. The King was wearing the uniform of Colonel-in-Chief of the Grenadier Guards.

While the Royal couple walked round the camp and chatted to the troops, a number of planes appeared and seemed to dive in salute to their Majesties.

The King and Queen – on their first and last visit to Derby together – then went on to Rolls-Royce, where they spent more than an hour.

"It gives us a fine and proud feeling to see our King and Queen moving about among us," remarked a foreman to a *Telegraph* reporter. "We shall go back to our jobs and redouble our efforts – if that is possible. I know it means a tremendous lot to men and girls."

The Royal couple went into the experimental department – from which photographers and reporters were excluded.

They also appeared on the balcony of the factory offices – where after the war, the part played by Rolls-Royce in the Battle of Britain was to be commemorated by the memorial window of stained glass.

"Hundreds of girls employed at a Derby factory engaged on war work 'mobbed' the Duke of Kent after he had toured the factory yesterday," the *Telegraph* reported on March 6, 1941.

"His Royal Highness was about to leave in his car when the girls swarmed out of offices and workshops and surrounded him.

"Many were in boiler suits and overalls their faces and hands grimy, but the Duke did not mind. They shook his hand and cheered him, and after officials and police had 'rescued' His Royal Highness, he consented to be photographed."

The visit was a great success with the Duke asking employees about working conditions, shifts, health and time off as he toured International Combustion.

He later moved on to E. W. Bliss & Co on City Road. The *Telegraph* commented: "Here, too, much of the work is done by girls who are particularly smart in blue overalls, caps and leather gloves – and lipstick, which one suspects was put on rather heavily in view of the occasion."

The Duke also met Home Guards, first aid and ARP personnel. He wore his RAF uniform and drove his own car on the visit. The Duke also spent some time looking at damage caused in Derby by air raids. Tragically, the following year the Duke was killed while on active service.

The Princess Royal, sister of King George VI and the Duke of Kent, made several war time visits to Derbyshire.

In March 1941 she visited an RAOC depot in Derby where she inspected ATS members. More than once she surprised them with her knowledge of their particular branch of the Service, the *Telegraph* recorded.

As Controller-Commandant of the ATS, the Princess was back again April 1944 for a repeat inspection where she showed great interest in the girls and their welfare.

The following year she visited Derbyshire Royal Infirmary and Ashe Hall Hospital, Etwall, to meet wounded soldiers who had seen the beginning of the German retreat in France.

In 1945, the Duchess of Kent visited Derby on a packed day of engagements which included trips to the Royal Crown Derby works, Ashe Hall Hospital and Rolls-Royce. She also opened the Red Cross Treasure Sale and St James's Street Salerooms.

The King and Queen arrive at Derby railway station on August 8, 1940.

Queen Elizabeth inspects troops at the Osmaston Camp, near Ashbourne.

Crowds wave and cheer as the King and Queen arrive at Derby railway station on August 8, 1940.

King George VI and the Indian troops – about 90 per cent of whom had served in frontier campaigns.

The King greets ex-servicemen during the tour of Rolls-Royce.

Young apprentices from Rolls-Royce cheered the Queen as she walked through the Rolls-Royce yard.

The King showed great interest in the work Rolls-Royce was carrying out.

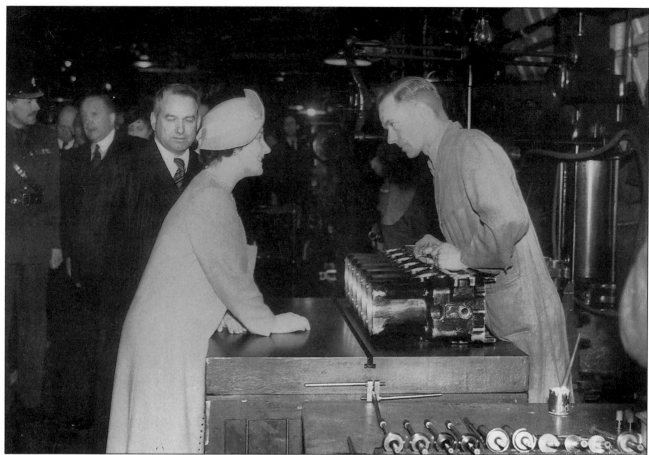

A high level of engineering knowledge was demonstrated by the Queen as she chatted to machine operators.

Merlin aero engines made by Rolls-Royce played a vital part in winning the Battle of Britain. Here, the King sees them in production.

All smiles as the Royal couple walk through lines of workers outside Rolls-Royce.

Kind words from the Queen for ex-servicemen outside Rolls-Royce.

Troops gave three rousing cheers for their Majesties at the end of the Rolls-Royce tour.

At Borough Police Headquarters in Derby, the Duke of Kent met civil defence workers on March 5, 1941.

Women's Auxiliary Police Corps members are inspected by the Duke.

Excited women workers "mobbed" the Duke, according to the *Telegraph*, when he left International Combustion.

Molly Chambers, working at E.W. Bliss & Co. was gently questioned by the Duke about her job.

The Princess Royal inspects ATS members during her visit to an R.A.O.C depot in Derby in March 1941.

A surprise visit to Rolls-Royce was made by the Duke and Duchess of Gloucester on March 11, 1943.

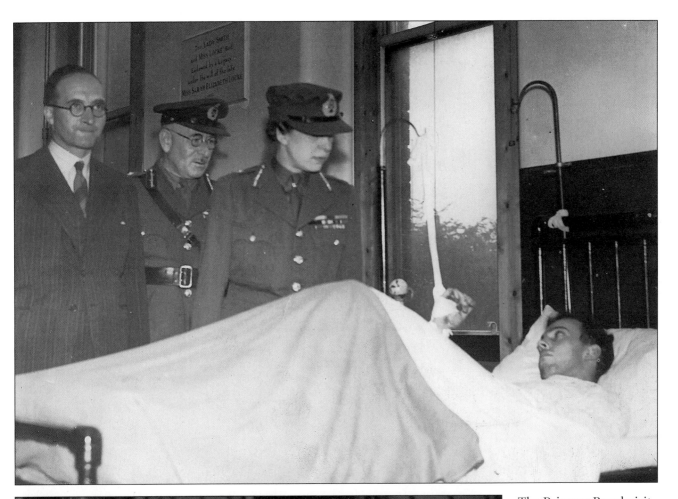

The Princess Royal visited Derbyshire Royal Infirmary twice in 1944. Here, during her September visit she spoke to practically every wounded man.

Pausing during her tour of Rolls-Royce in July 1945, the Duchess of Kent watched the work of one operator closely.

Chapter Three

From Princess to Queen

HIGH up on the Council House in Derby is carved MCMXLI – which to those who can decipher Roman numerals is 1941.

But it was on Monday 27 June 1949 that Princess Elizabeth – and her husband, the Duke of Edinburgh – came to officially open the building.

Work began on the Council House in July 1938 and was scheduled for completion in 1941 – but the outbreak of World War Two brought work to a standstill for a while.

It was a day of blazing sunshine when the Royal couple arrived. The Princess wore a green and white checked taffeta dress with full skirt, fitted bodice and a bow at the waist. Her bonnet-shaped hat in natural straw was decorated with Lilies-of-the-Valley. The Duke looked bronzed following a trip to the Channel Islands.

The couple were met at Darley Park just before 4pm by the Mayor, and various civic dignitaries were introduced to them.

From the Park, the entourage drove down Duffield Road to the town centre.

At the Royal Crown Derby china works the Royal couple went their separate ways. While the Princess toured the factory the Duke went on to Rolls-Royce.

Princess Elizabeth met many long serving employees including Emma Braine, of Davenport Road, who had worked at Crown Derby for 52 years and had helped to decorate a tea set for the Princess and her sister, Princess Margaret, when they were young.

After signing the visitors book, the Princess was given a christening mug painted with Prince Charles' name and his date of birth.

Meanwhile, at Rolls-Royce, the Duke turned into No 2 gate to walk the 300 yards to the fitting and erecting shop.

The *Telegraph* reported how watching men applauded and women cheered.

"Oh girls, look at that smile," was one comment from a group of women sitting on an air raid shelter.

The Duke spoke to many employees including Mr C. E. Stone of Becket Well Lane, a veteran of World War One who was awarded the VC in 1918 for his courage in saving his guns from capture by the Germans.

Mr Stone, who had worked at Rolls-Royce since 1924, had previously met King George VI and Queen Elizabeth on their 1940 visit and the Duke of Windsor.

When the Princess rejoined the Duke at Rolls-Royce they admired the Battle of Britain memorial window before leaving for the Council House.

A silver gilt key was given to the Princess to open the main doors. She was greeted by the sight of huge banks of flowers in the main hall.

There were more Royal Crown Derby gifts for the couple, this time china dessert dishes to match the dinner and tea services sent to them from Derby as a wedding present.

After tea at the Council House, the couple waved to the waiting crowds from the balcony before leaving for the war memorial site at Allenton where the Princess laid the foundation stone for the war memorial village for disabled ex-servicemen.

The Princess gave a moving speech praising Derby for the wisdom and imagination of the decision to build such a development.

She told her audience: "In years to come when my husband and I revisit the town we shall look forward to finding at this place a flourishing community where the fallen are not forgotten and where the debt we owe to them is paid in service to the new generation.

"When, as this evening, we stand united in the recollection of those who gave all they had for us – and pray God to make us worthy of their example – our own quarrels and complaints, and our daily worries shrink into insignificance and we are left with a truer sense of values."

The visit ended when the Royal couple caught a train from Derby railway station at 7.45pm.

No-one expected then, that less than three years later this Princess would be Queen following the sudden death of her father in the 16th year of his reign, aged just 57.

The 25-year-old Princess was on a Commonwealth tour of Africa when the King died on Wednesday February 6, 1952.

In Derby, the Mayor, Councillor Z.P. Grayson read the proclamation that Elizabeth was Queen, from the steps of the Council House.

When the Queen was crowned in Westminster Abbey on June 2, 1953, photographs of the day's events were flown to the *Derby Telegraph* for publication the same day. Every street in the town seemed to have planned a street party. Some went ahead, despite the rain while others delayed their celebrations for a day.

Some 22,000 Derby school children had a half day holiday on March 28, 1957, when the Queen made her first visit to the town as Sovereign.

Arriving at Sudbury station at 10am, the Queen and the Duke of Edinburgh had a number of engagements around Burton upon Trent and Tutbury before arriving at Repton School for lunch and an afternoon of tours and ceremonies.

At 4pm the Queen arrived in Derby Market Place and inspected a Guard of Honour.

Afterwards, the Queen visited The Leylands Estate, Broadway, the Woollen Drapers' Cottage Homes, where she signed a Book of Remembrance, inspected a flat, the nursing wing, rest home and chapel while the Duke went to the Leicestershire and Derbyshire Yeomanry depot on Siddals Road, Derby.

The Royal couple met up again for tea at the Council House, where Derby Corporation presented them with another Royal Crown Derby dinner service. At Chaddesden the couple planted trees at St Philip's, Taddington Road, before leaving from Spondon station.

The *Derby Evening Telegraph* special picture edition produced on Friday July 1, 1949.

Two studies indicating the keen interest that was shown by the Princess as she inspected the skilled craftsmanship of employees during her visit to the Royal Crown Derby works.

The Princess and the Duke ack crowd from the balcony of the visitors arriving at the Counci

The Duke carrying out his inspection of a guard of honour at the Memorial Village site.

Scene inside the reception room at the Council House. In the forefront of the picture can be seen the visitors' book and the gift to the royal visitors of Crown Derby china dessert dishes.

Mrs. R. Bryn Owen, who, as the daughter of Alderman A. E. Moult, frequently deputised for her mother as Mayoress of Derby during Alderman Moult's term of office, being presented to the Princess at the Council House.

The Princess expressed great pleasure at the gesture of the ma bearing the name of Prince Charles. After the royal visit right, Councillor Alec Ling, Mr. A. K. Haslehurst, Mrs. G. F. Arthu

DERBY EVENING TELEGRAPH, FRIDAY, JULY 1, 1949   7

Chatting with Mr. J. M. Garrow, Chief Constable of Derbyshire, at the Memorial Village site are (left to right) Mrs. Noel-Baker, Mr. P. J. Noel-Baker, M.P. for Derby, Mrs. Wilcock and Group-Captain C. A. B. Wilcock, M.P. for Derby. BELOW: To make sure of getting a good view, a visitor to the Memorial Village site uses his binoculars.

Mr. E. W. Hives, managing director of Rolls-Royce, steps forward to be presented to the Duke by the Deputy Mayor of Derby (Councillor G. F. War-burton) outside the works.

The Princess inspecting a contingent of ex-Servicemen.

The Princess with the Mayor and Mayoress of Derby at the Memorial Village site.

Another section of the crowd at the Memorial Village site.

Derby works in presenting to her two replicas of the Derbyshire dwarfs (on table) and a christening mug guests to see the display which had earlier been admired by the Princess. In the picture (left) are, left to) (holding the christening mug), Mrs. Gilbert Moult, Mrs. Ling, and Mrs. Haslehurst. RIGHT: Councillor Walker (right). At the back is Councillor M. F. Milne.

The *Derby Evening Telegraph* special picture edition centre pages.

47

Flags were out in St Peter's Street to mark the visit of Princess Elizabeth on June 27, 1949.

The Princess smiles happily with the Mayor of Derby, Alderman C.F. Bowmer.

On her visit to Royal Crown Derby, the Princess showed great interest in the production process.

The Princess watched china being decorated by hand on her tour of Royal Crown Derby accompanied by the Chairman of the Directors, Mr H.T. Robinson.

Ex-servicemen are inspected by Princess Elizabeth.

A bright but formal outfit in green and white taffeta was the choice of the young Princess.

Princess Elizabeth and the Duke of Edinburgh spend several moments in contemplation of the Battle of Britain memorial window at Rolls-Royce.

The Royal couple arrive at the Council House to officially open it.

DERBY EVENING TELEGRAPH, FEBRUARY 6, 1952

DERBY EVENING TELEGRAPH

EXTRA SPECIAL

INCORPORATING THE DERBY DAILY EXPRESS

No. 21,976   WEDNESDAY, FEBRUARY 6, 1952   TWOPENCE

Nation and world stunned by Sandringham news

THE KING DIES PEACEFULLY IN HIS SLEEP

THE KING is dead. He passed away peacefully in his sleep at Sandringham early this morning. He was in his 57th year and the 16th year of his reign.

The news, which was announced from Sandringham at 10.45 a.m., stunned the nation and the world. Princess Elizabeth is now Queen. This is the first time in history that a British Sovereign has acceded to the Throne while in Africa.

HIS LAST FAREWELL

One of the last pictures of the King as he waved farewell to Princess Elizabeth and the Duke of Edinburgh.

In best of health yesterday

THE KING, the Sandringham announcement stated, appeared to be in his usual health when he retired last night.

Earlier in the day he had been out both during the morning and afternoon and to everybody he appeared to be in the very best of health.

The Queen and Princess Margaret are at Sandringham at present. The tragic news was immediately given to Mr. Churchill and the Home Secretary by telephone and an emergency Cabinet meeting was called.

The King died where he was born—at Sandringham—though it was in the earlier York Cottage in the grounds near the big house that his birth took place on December 4, 1895.

His father, King George V., also died at Sandringham—16 years ago, on January 21, 1936.

Queen Mary was informed at Marlborough House. It is understood that she intends to remain there and will not be travelling to Sandringham.

The doctor who was called this morning was Dr. James Ansell, Surgeon Apothecary to the Household at Sandringham. Members of the Household staying at Sandringham were Sir Alan Lascelles, the King's Private Secretary; Sir Harold Campbell, the King's Equerry; and Lady Hyde, Lady-in-Waiting to the Queen.

PRIVY COUNCIL MEETING

The Privy Council will be held at St. James's Palace later to-day. The Council is automatically summoned on the death of the King and is traditionally known as the Accession Council.

It is at this meeting that the Lords of the Privy Council accept the new Sovereign "as their Lawful Rightful Liege Lord." They also agree to the wording of the proclamation of the new monarch.

Telegrams summoning them to the meeting were sent from the Privy Council offices in Whitehall to all councillors this morning. The total number of Councillors is more than 300, but only a few will be available for to-day's meeting.

Both Houses of Parliament formally adjourned this afternoon until to-night when the re-swearing in of Members will commence.

Turn to back page

NEW QUEEN IS FLYING HOME

ELIZABETH, the new Queen, was told to-day of her father's death when she returned to the Royal Lodge at Nyeri in Kenya, where she was to spend the day resting. On hearing the news she burst into tears. She immediately decided to fly back to London to-day and will arrive at London Airport at 4.30 p.m. to-morrow.

DERBY VISIT

THE NEW QUEEN photographed on her visit to Derby in June, 1949.

The aircraft Atalanta awaited her and the Duke of Edinburgh at Mombasa Airport.

Elizabeth and the Duke had just come back from the "Tree-tops Hotel" from which, by artificial moonlight, they looked down on jungle animals in their wild environment.

The royal couple came back happily to the lodge, totally unprepared for the blow that was to befall them.

Call to Palace

The news was at first withheld from them until hard confirmation was obtained.

A newspaper, the "East African Standard," gave the first news to the staff at the Royal Lodge. Not until a direct radio telephone call had been made to Buckingham Palace and the tragic news confirmed from there, was the Princess told that the King was dead and she herself was the reigning Queen of England.

In an instant all the elaborate plans for their tour fell to the ground. In the midst of sorrow they had to prepare their minds for vast new responsibilities.

The liner Gothic which was to have taken them to Ceylon lies idle at Mombasa, her flag at half-mast and her crew disconsolate.

17-hour trip

B.O.A.C. arranged by telephone from London for the same 'plane which took the royal couple to Nairobi to stand by to fly them back. The total journey to London will take about 17 hours.

The Atalanta has been re-stocked and will fly via Entebbe, Uganda, and El Adem on the North African coast where it will refuel. It will pick up a fresh crew at El Adem and then fly non-stop to London Airport.

Derby is shocked by tragic news

NEWS of the King's death came as a severe shock in Derby. Groups formed in the streets, discussing the news in shocked amazement.

The comment of one woman to a "Telegraph" reporter—"I feel quite stunned"—summed up the reaction of Derby people to the tragic loss of their Sovereign.

Members of Derby Town Council stood in silence to-day before agreeing to defer the business to a date to be fixed by the Mayor (Councillor Z. P. Grayson).

The Council decided to present an address of loyalty, which included an expression of sympathy on the death of her father, to Queen Elizabeth, and an address of condolence to the Queen Mother.

(See Pictures in Page 12.)

EMPIRE MOURNS WITH BRITAIN

SHOCK and a sense of sudden loss were the predominant feelings in the Empire and abroad as news of the death of the King circulated in the streets, offices and remote areas of the world.

World statesmen immediately began to prepare their condolences to the Royal Family and the British people.

Reuter messages from the capitals said:—

Paris: President Vincent Auriol immediately sent a courier to the British Embassy and sat down to write a telegram to the Queen. It was assumed that the President would represent France at the funeral.

In South Africa sorrow was deepened by the fact that the people had been looking forward to the King's visit.

Deep sympathy was expressed for Princess Elizabeth at the blow which has overtaken her while enjoying her stay in East Africa. The South African Broadcasting Corporation stopped its broadcasts to announce the news.

Mr. Sidney Holland, New Zealand Prime Minister, who is visiting Berlin and West Germany, said he would probably delay his return to New Zealand. He may return to London to-morrow. Mr. Holland learned of the King's death while in the officers' mess of the Durham Light Infantry in Berlin.

IN THE U.S.
The news of the King's death reached the United States in the early morning hours as most of the nation slept.

First pre-dawn bulletins of the event were broadcast over all-night radio stations.

The British Forces Radio network flashed the news to all His Majesty's Forces in Germany and then closed down in tribute.

General Eisenhower ordered all the flags at his headquarters near Paris to be lowered. The flags of the 12 North Atlantic Treaty Nations went down to half mast within minutes after the news reached S.H.A.P.E.

In Italy Pope Pius was informed immediately by Mr. Walter St. C. H. Roberts, the British Ambassador to the Holy See. The Pontiff instructed that a telegram of condolence be sent at once to the Royal family.

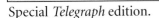

Derby people view the wreath being sent to King George VI's funeral in the Council House.

The *Derby Evening Telegraph* offices, then on Albert Street, were decorated for the Coronation of Queen Elizabeth II.

In 1957, at Repton School, there was a chance to reminisce about the Coronation four years earlier when the Queen met up with Lord Fisher, former headmaster of Repton School and Chairman of its governing body, who as Archbishop of Canterbury had crowned her.

A radiant smile from the Queen as she accepts a bouquet of roses during her 1957 visit.

The Queen inspects a Guard of Honour in Derby Market Place.

A joke from the Duke at the Leicestershire and Derbyshire Yeomanry depot on Siddals Road, Derby.

Close inspection of one veteran's medals when the Duke of Edinburgh visited the Yeomanry depot.

Crowds of Derbyshire Brownies made sure of a good seat early on the Royal route.

Excited youngsters wave homemade decorations as they wait to catch a glimpse of their Queen.

A Royal walkabout by Queen Elizabeth at the Leylands Estate, Broadway.

Residents and staff are introduced to the Queen at the Leylands Estate.

A regal wave from the balcony of the Council House which the Queen had officially opened eight years earlier.

It had been a hectic day of engagements, with plenty for the Royal couple to reflect upon.

The Royal couple were delighted by the warmth of their welcome in 1957.

Chapter Four

The Sixties – and a Royal Boost for Derby's Industries

PERHAPS it was a hangover from Beatle-mania and the excitement of the 1960s pop scene, but teenage girls screamed a welcome when the Duke of Edinburgh arrived at Derby railway station for a two-day visit on May 14, 1964.

His first stop was at the Locomotive Works Training School, where Dr Richard Beeching – Chairman of British Railways Board – was presented to him.

Later, a cheer went up in Derby Loco Works when the Duke couldn't resist slipping into the driver's seat of a new diesel locomotive being built and taking the controls with a broad grin.

When he came to open the new £1.25-million British Railways engineering research laboratories in London Road, the Duke told his audience he was convinced that British Railways would emerge as the most efficient transport system anywhere.

"There is no doubt whatever, in my mind, that once British people have a well-organised show to run, they run it more efficiently than anyone else in the world," he said.

"We all know that it happens to be fashionable just now to make fun of British Railways. The complaints, the accusations and the jokes which are bandied about with such splendid irrelevance are enough to make the most patient and long-suffering railwayman feel rather fed up."

The Duke continued by saying he believed railways were "over the hump" and the new laboratories were "symbolic of the new sense of urgency and promise which was infecting the whole service."

After lunch at the Midland Hotel, the Duke went on to formally open new buildings at the Derby Diocesan Training College in Mickleover.

"How anyone has the face even to start to train as a teacher beats me," he joked.

"Qualities needed by teachers are the patience of a bird watcher, the sympathy of parents and the leadership of a general. Then they are expected to take on every extra chore."

He couldn't resist remarking that his own Duke of Edinburgh Award Scheme had probably saddled teachers with yet another task.

The Duke congratulated the designers of the building and added: "I also wish all the inmates the best of luck and offer sympathy and congratulations to the staff."

On behalf of the students, Mr G. C. Dredge – President of the Students' Union – presented the Duke with a £150 cheque for the National Playing Fields Association.

Among the students the Duke met were Marion Hine, Keith Davies and Roger Holland who had all won Silver Duke of Edinburgh Awards.

On the playing fields the Duke took particular interest in a boat built by Olive Petticrew of Birkenhead. He asked her if it leaked, and when she said it did, he smiled and offered some advice, which went unrecorded by the Telegraph.

The Duke was 25 minutes behind schedule for his next stop at St John's Church, Mickleover.

He took great interest in the Duke of Edinburgh Award Scheme activities of 15-year-old Keith Byrne of 84 Brisbane Road and 16-year-old David Brinklow of 5 Murray Road, both members of the church's youth club.

There was also time for a word with local Guides and Scouts and a moment's contemplation of the church's unusual architecture before leaving for Okeover Hall.

After spending the night as a guest of the Lord Lieutenant of Derbyshire, Sir Ian Walker-Okeover, the Duke continued next day with his busy schedule. He opened the £2.5-million Derby and District Colleges of Art and Technology on Kedleston Road. He toured the building and met staff and more students who had gained Duke of Edinburgh Awards.

In the afternoon he rounded off the visit by seeing the new lido at Alfreton.

In 1965 it was the turn of Rolls-Royce to receive the Royal seal of approval from the Duke. He spent three hours at the company's works at Sinfin and Raynesway in November that year.

In the test department at Sinfin, Prince Philip watched equipment which could evaluate the performance of engines up to speeds of 2.5 times that of sound and at heights of 70,000 feet.

In March 1969, the Duke was back in Derby where he met more people connected with his awards scheme during a hectic 75-minute visit to Mackworth Secondary School and Markeaton Park.

The Princess Royal, who made several morale-boosting visits to the town during the war, was back in April 1963 to lend support to the Derby YMCA Building Fund Appeal towards the cost of new headquarters. Her visit came 12 days after the Duke of Gloucester opened Merlin Boys' Club in Osmaston Road.

A Royal Crown Derby dish was presented to the Princess Royal by Miss Wendy Dalton when the Royal guest went to Derby Playhouse to receive donations towards the building fund which then stood at £41,000.

Princess Margaret, who had married Lord Snowdon at the start of the decade, made a couple of visits to Derby in the 1960s. On a grey November day she called in at Bemrose & Sons printing works in Spondon.

She wore a black, loose-fitting coat with a wide black collar and a dome-shaped hat of black and white fur. As she toured the factory, about 250 employees crowded into a marquee in the yard to catch a glimpse of the Princess as she walked between the departments. Girls from the fourth form of Spondon House Secondary School were among those waiting in the cold and rain.

After the Bemrose tour, the Princess's car drove her through Derby. Near St Mary's Bridge, the *Telegraph* reported, she got a "teenage reception of squeals and cries of Yeah, Yeah, Yeah!"

Tradition triumphed when a workman in over-alls came out of Derby Power Station with a rather tattered Union Flag which he propped against some railings with the remark, "Someone's got to make an effort."

Two years later the weather again played havoc with a visit by the Queen's sister. Princess Margaret was going to inspect nearly 6,000 St John Ambulance Cadets outside Bemrose School on July 11, 1965 – but torrential rain meant everyone crammed into the school and the visit took place in tightly-packed classrooms.

The Princess came as Commandant-in-Chief of St John Ambulance and wore her official uniform. The tour was much more informal than it would have been outside, with an enrolment ceremony and presentation of badges.

In June 1966, the Princess's husband – Lord Snowdon – visited Joseph Bourne & Son pottery at Derby before moving on to Royal Crown Derby.

Some 16 months earlier, Lord Snowdon had visited the borough in his professional capacity of *Sunday Times* photographer to complete a picture feature on mixed marriages. His principal subjects were world mid-heavyweight weight-lifting champion Louis Martin and his bride Ann, who had posed at their Rawdon Street home in New Normanton.

Prince Philip opens the £1.25-million British Railway Engineering Research Laboratories on London Road.

The Duke is accompanied by Mr T. F. B. Simpson, loco works manager, with Dr Richard Beeching – Chairman of British Railways Board – behind him. There was plenty of chance for souvenir snaps by amateur photographers in the workforce.

On his way out from St John's Church, Mickleover, the Duke stopped for a word with Mr T. M. Brown, District Scout Commissioner for Derby North. Close behind the Duke is the Revd Martin Pierce, Vicar of St John's.

The Duke at Alfreton Lido at the end of his two-day visit in May 1964.

At Rolls-Royce in 1965, the Duke looked at Spey Turbine Blade parts at Sinfin Works.

Miss Rita Pearson was "thrilled to bits" when the Duke made a detour from his official programme to speak to her and a colleague in the Vibration and Strain Gauge Laboratory. "What a fiddling job," he remarked.

A rites of Spring Leap was performed for the Duke at Mackworth School in 1969 by folk dancers Markham Singh (left) and Tom Cross.

At Mackworth School, the Duke looked at many displays by youngsters following his award scheme, including one on Origami – the art of paper folding.

Mayor of Derby, Councillor Stuart Harpur, welcomes the Princess Royal outside the Council House. On the left is Sir Ian Walker- Okeover, Lord Lieutenant of Derbyshire.

The Princess Royal and the Mayor arrive at Derby Playhouse where the Princess accepted donations for the YMCA building fund in April 1963.

Mrs Peggy Elkes, a rewinding operative explains her work to the Princess at the Bemrose factory in Spondon, in November 1963.

A rare break in the rain during Princess Margaret's 1965 visit enabled her to walk through a line of St John Ambulance cadets. With her is Captain P. J. B. Drury-Lowe, the St John County Commissioner.

The Princess signs in at the Council House, watched by the Mayor of Derby, Councillor William Bonell.

Thousands of cadets crammed inside Bemrose School for inspections and presentations by Princess Margaret – their Commander-in-Chief. Here, she presents a bravery award – The American Cup for Gallantry – to 15-year-old Hugh Kenneth Williams of the Cynwyd Ambulance Cadet Division in Wales.

Lord Snowdon visited Royal Crown Derby in June 1966 as part of a three-day tour of potteries in his capacity as Consultant to the Council of Industrial Design. Here he looks at a 24cwt gold raised decoration with Mr Albert Haddock, the senior gilder who had been with the company for 64 years.

Chapter Five

A Touch of Glamour

DERBY'S Royal highspot of the 1970s was undoubtedly the Queen's visit in 1977 to declare Derby a city. But plenty of other visits kept Derby people cheered up in a decade which saw some belt-tightening as the recession hit home.

Conscious of the state of the economy, the Queen Mother turned down a costly gift of Royal Crown Derby porcelain china when she came to open the Assembly Rooms on November 9, 1977. Several weeks before the visit, when plans were being finalised, the Queen Mother said that although she appreciated the thought behind the gift she thought it would be inappropriate to accept given the country's economic difficulties. She opted instead for another much less costly piece of china, the Mayor of Derby, Councillor Jeffery Tillett revealed.

On the night of the opening, with a concert by the Royal Philharmonic Orchestra of which the Queen Mother was patron, admission prices were hoisted to £1.50, £2.50 and £3.50. Concert proceeds of £1,000 were sent to the Queen's Jubilee Appeal.

The 77-year-old Queen Mother brought a touch of West End gala-night glamour to Derby when she stepped from the Royal Rolls-Royce in a turquoise and silver satin dress with a shawl collar, a diamond tiara, diamond and pearl necklace and white mink.

Councillor Tillett, handing over the favoured gift of a Royal Crown Derby loving cup, told her Majesty: "You hold a special place in the hearts of the British people, and the people of Derby, who give you their love and loyalty."

During the concert interval, the Queen Mother mingled with councillors and local businessmen. She shocked Mrs Betty Betts, outside catering manager for Ansells Brewery in Derby, who served her with a gin and Dubonnet, by recalling their previous meeting at the 1976 East of England Show. "I was amazed she remembered me," said Mrs Betts.

Afterwards, the Queen Mother mingled with enthusiastic concert goers before making the short trip across the road to the Council House. The following day, she opened St Christopher's Railway Home on Ashbourne Road. Protocol also took a back seat six years earlier, when the Queen Mother spent five hours in Derby visiting Royal Crown Derby, having lunch at the Council House, and touring the Guildhall and Derby Cathedral.

Mayor of Derby, Councillor Joe Carty said afterwards that she was delighted by the reception she received and had told him, "I never expected such a turn out."

During her walkabout she patted police horse Little John, and commented "What a fine fellow". She also had cheery words and friendly pats for two-year-old twins Kevin and Paul Ronchi of 14 Pittar Street, Derby.

At the Council House, the Queen Mother stopped at the entrance to admire the beautiful flower arrangements. She was so impressed that she asked for a geranium cutting. Councillor L.L. MacDonald, chairman of the Parks Committee, offered an entire plant which was later put in one of the Royal cars. Other planned gifts that day in June 1971 were a Royal Crown Derby bowl, a Joseph Wright drawing and a book of photographs of old Derby.

On November 24, 1970, the Duke of Edinburgh made a return trip to the British Railways laboratories on London Road which he had opened in 1964. Because of the secrecy surrounding much of the work there, the visit was semi-private.

At a new £250,000 advanced projects laboratory opened the previous month, the Duke saw work on the 150mph advanced passenger train.

Princess Anne threw back her head and roared with laughter during a 1974 visit to Royal Crown Derby when works director Mr A. Rigby jumped up and down on a Crown Derby plate to demonstrate its toughness. Security was tight throughout the visit and the Princess's bodyguard – Detective Inspector Jim Beaton – was never far from her side.

The previous day he had been invested with the George Cross for his bravery during the attempted kidnapping of the Princess on the Mall, in London, earlier that year.

The Princess wore a light weight wool suit in coral with a cream figured shirt, brown velour hat, and patent shoes.

Six plates presented to the Princess at the end of her visit were later given by her as prizes at a ball in aid of the Save the Children fund.

New premises for the Royal School for the Deaf

on Ashbourne Road were officially opened by Princess Margaret on June 28, 1973. She also visited the Rycote Centre on Kedleston Road. Wearing a tomato red coat and a bright green hat she received gifts for her children made by pupils at the Royal School for the Deaf.

The Princess seemed most fascinated by the primary and nursery departments where she spent 15 minutes with pupils and staff. She was delighted to receive a single flower and a book – *Alphabet of Flowers* – from three-year-old pupil Emma Mills. "Oh, one of my favourite books," the Princess exclaimed.

After cocktails at the Council House, the Princess arrived at the Rycote Centre to be met by Councillor Bill Pritchard, chairman of Derby Town Council and Social Services, who explained that 376 people visited the centre daily throughout the week. He invited the Princess to choose a gift from a selection of articles made at Rycote, and she selected a turquoise cuddly dog, playfully pulling its long tongue before handing it to her lady-in-waiting.

Princess Alice, Duchess of Gloucester, called into Derby Cathedral in August 1979 – after attending the gala opening of Buxton Festival – to view a national embroidery exhibition.

November 26, 1972 was a day to remember for hundreds of Red Cross workers thanks to Princess Alexandra. She opened the £24,000 headquarters of the Derby Borough Division of the British Red Cross Society in Liversage Street before visiting Spondon School to present awards to the winning teams at a regional Red Cross junior competition.

Wearing a red and green flared tartan coat, with a scarlet turban-style hat, Princess Alexandra dispensed with formality completely and mingled with the crowds for a friendly chat. At Liversage Street, the Princess – as vice president of the Red Cross and Patron of the junior Red Cross – remarked: "To care for your neighbour is the very essence of the Red Cross and this spirit abounds in Derby."

In Spondon, about 500 cadets from Derbyshire and neighbouring counties were taking part in the regional competition. The Derbyshire teams won five of the nine sections and the county tied with North Lincolnshire for the highest overall points total.

In November 1975, Princess Alexandra returned to tour Derby Playhouse and the Derbyshire Royal Infirmary. A highlight of her visit was a laugh and a chat with 105-year-old Mrs Fanny Berry who could remember the Princess's great-grandmother Queen Victoria laying the foundation stone of the Infirmary in 1891.

Amazingly – Mrs Berry was still going strong four years later when Prince Charles was her "Darling" and made her dream come true. The *Derby Evening Telegraph* had revealed in its Centenary Special that Mrs Berry had put Prince Charles top of her birthday guest list.

A couple from Spondon brought the article to the attention of the Palace. So it was, that when Charles visited Derbyshire's first Festival of Remembrance at the Assembly Rooms – one week before Mrs Berry's 109th birthday – he also spent almost an hour at Warwick House Old People's Home in Bonsall Avenue, Littleover.

For 20 minutes he talked solely to Mrs Berry, remarking that her birthday was two days before his and adding: "Of course all the best people are born in November." He told her how at the Festival of Remembrance – organised by the County Committee of the Royal British Legion – he had met an old soldier of 101. "It must be the Derbyshire air, everyone looks so fit," said the Prince.

Mrs Berry insisted on standing to greet the Prince, then they chatted about their families and Mrs Berry told him how she had seen Queen Victoria and met Princess Alexandra. Afterwards she said: "It was such an honour to have him here. He's a delightful young man, a charmer, and he'll make a grand King. Of course, he's been very well brought up. He has very good parents."

The Prince had a word with all the home's 49 residents – and even a goldfish in a tank in the hall. His visit had started at the Cathedral where he viewed Bess of Hardwick's tomb and a monument marking Bonnie Prince Charlie's visit.

At the Festival of Remembrance, 109 Standards were massed colourfully at the back of the stage. Taking part were Mickleover Legion Pipe Band, Allestree Royal British Legion Glee Club, City of Derby Youth Band and the Regimental Band of the Cheshire Regiment. Religious leaders of all denominations also took part.

A glimpse of the fashions of the days as a young Princess Anne arrives at East Midlands Airport on June 23, 1970, for a visit to Nottinghamshire. Girls' Venture Corps members from Derbyshire were among the guard of honour.

The Duke of Edinburgh discusses railway operating movements with Mr H. Potts, Derby Area Manager, British Railways, in the Derby power signal box which controls 178 miles of track. This was during the Duke's visit on November 24, 1970.

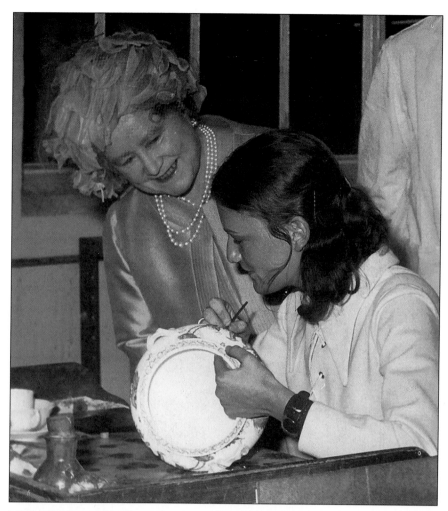

Pausing for a word with one of the workers at Royal Crown Derby, the Queen Mother admires her painstaking handiwork.

The Queen Mother holds up the China bowl she was presented with to mark her tour of Royal Crown Derby in June 1971.

DERBY EVENING TELEGRAPH, Wednesday, June 9, 1971

'WALKABOUT' BY QUEEN MOTHER

PROTOCOL took a back seat during yesterday's visit of the Queen Elizabeth Queen Mother to Derby. True to today's trends within the Royal Family, she became one of the "walkabout" Royals.

During an arduous tour of the Royal Crown Derby Porcelain Co. Ltd., she stepped out of line on numerous occasions and sprung surprises on many of the employees by chatting to them about their work.

And on her walk from the Council House to the Guildhall she spoke to members of the crowds lining the route — and even had a friendly word with a police horse, Little John, ridden by Police-constable Richard Tuska, of the Nottinghamshire Combined Constabulary.

ENTHUSIASTIC

From the minute she stepped inside the works of the Royal Crown Derby Porcelain Co. Ltd., the Queen Mother took an enthusiastic interest in every aspect of the production of the china pieces.

Among those she spoke to were Mrs. Marjorie Spencer, of 102 Holbrook Road, Alvaston, who puts handles on cups; Mrs. Doreen Sheldon, of 72 Meadow Lane, Chaddesden; and Mrs. Nora Waumsley, of 133 Perth Street, Derby.

In the casting department Mr. Arthur Ussher, of 24 Alexandra Street, Derby, showed her how to cast a cream jug and watched as she did so.

She admired the work of figure maker Mrs. Maria Franckiewz, of 16 Gerard Street, Derby, and of Mrs. Dorothy Mortimer, flower maker, of 22a Madison Avenue, Chaddesden.

WHAT A WASTE

The Queen Mother also expressed interest in the work of Mrs. Glenys Alton, of 21 Border Crescent, Alvaston, and Mrs. Peggy Dyer of 16 Sidney Street, Derby, and said to Mrs. Doris Robinson, examiner supervisor, on seeing some rejects: "Oh dear, what a waste to smash them."

Mrs. Marlene Rose, of 64 Street Lane, Denby, and Mrs. Margaret Kirk, of 67 Pear Tree Road, Derby, were both nervous

and thrilled when she spoke to them.

She told Mr. John Aldridge, manager of the glost department: "People don't realise just what work goes into making Crown Derby china."

She also met gilders, lithographers and enamellers, secretaries and guides, and truck emptier Mr. Victor Thorpe, of 3 Kingsmead Close, Derby.

PRESENTATION

One of the highlights of her visit was a presentation of a fruit basket to Miss Mary Ellen Murray, a burnisher at the works for 58 years, who claims she has no thoughts of retirement yet, although she is 72 years old.

"It made my day," she exclaimed after a five-minute chat with the Queen Mother. "I never thought it would happen to me."

The Queen Mother asked her all about the process of the china finishing department, and said how much she had enjoyed her visit.

Crowds lined the streets, waving and cheering as the Royal entourage made its way to the Council House for the official lunch. The steps to the main entrance were banked with flowers grown and displayed by Derby Corporation Parks Department.

MUTUAL INTEREST

Once inside the Council House, the Queen Mother was introduced to the luncheon guests and found she shared a mutual interest in salmon fishing with Estates Department manager, Mr. F. G. Durant.

"We were talking first of all about Scotland; then salmon fishing cropped up, so I waded in," said Mr. Durant, who says he once caught one weighing 26½lb.

Until she retired to the Mayor's Parlour before lunch, the Queen Mother kept well to time schedule; but she was nearly half-an-hour late leaving

the Council House after a civic lunch in the Reception Room, and by then the crowds had built up on the Council House steps and along her path to the Guildhall.

She emerged from the Council House to a cheering, waving crowd of housewives, babies in arms, and schoolchildren, and waived the time lag to one side as she walked slowly through a police cordon.

On the way she stopped several times, talking to people in the crowd.

YOUNG TWINS

She had a cheery word for two-year-old brown-eyed twins Kevin and Paul Ronchi, of 14 Pittar Street, Derby; and Julie Anderson and Alan Brannon, to whom she gave a friendly pat.

As she neared the Guildhall entrance, she strayed away from the official party, patted police horse Little John, and commented: "What a fine fellow."

Closed circuit television cameras were inside the Guildhall so that those sitting in the auditorium could see her as she mounted the stairs, and entered the auditorium, and while she looked round the exhibition of photographs of old Derby, and paintings, afterwards.

As she took her seat on the platform in readiness for the official opening, eight-year-old Angela Betts, daughter of Alderman and Mrs. A. D. C. Betts, presented her with a posy of roses.

She gave a delightful curtsy, and the Queen Mother was later heard to comment: "She was a sweet little girl. She did it beautifully."

In her speech, the Queen Mother said: "I am indeed happy to have the opportunity of coming here today and I am so glad that this occasion should mark the triumphant conclusion of a scheme for the restoration of one of Derby's most notable monuments."

DEMOLITIONS

"From many parts of our country one hears almost daily that old buildings of historic interest are being demolished. Some have outlived their purpose, some stand in the way of new development plans, and others can no longer be maintained by their owners and fall into decay.

"But whatever the reason,

a little bit of our natural heritage is lost each time an old building disappears from the landscape.

"It is therefore most encouraging that this beautiful Guildhall should have been restored and redesigned as a concert and lecture hall and I trust that it may once again become a focal point for the borough's many activities. I congratulate most warmly all those who have been responsible for the planning of this venture and who, by work of brain or hand, have helped towards its completion.

The Queen Mother then thanked Alderman C. E. J. Andrews for a gift he presented to her of a Joseph Wright drawing, and said: "It will always remind me of my visit here and of the kind and loyal welcome I have received from the citizens of this ancient town."

EXHIBITIONS

After the opening, she toured an exhibition of photographs of old Derby and of other historical relics associated with the town.

These included a copy of July 1, 1949, souvenir edition of the Telegraph, commemorating the visit of the Queen, then Princess Elizabeth, and the Duke of Edinburgh, to Derby on June 27.

Councillor L. L. Macdonald then presented her with a bound book of copies of photographs in the exhibition. To her Lady-in-Waiting, who had been holding the posy presented earlier, the Queen Mother handed over the book, took the posy and said: "We'll swop now, shall we?"

She was escorted round the exhibition by the Borough Librarian, Mr. R. E. Marston, and earlier was introduced to Mr. N. G. Rushton, general manager of the Baths and Entertainments Department.

After looking at the commemoration plaque on her way down the Guildhall stairs, the Queen Mother then inspected an exhibition of Joseph Wright paintings on the ground floor.

Once more, the crowds were out in full as the royal cars

made their way up Irongate to Derby Cathedral, where she was received by the Bishop of Derby, the Rt. Rev. Cyril Bowles.

Before a conducted tour of the Cathedral, she met Mrs. Bowles, the Provost (the Very Rev. R. A. Beddoes) and Mrs. Beddoes; the Ven. J. F. Richardson (Archdeacon of Derby) and Mrs. Richardson, and Canon Paul Miller.

She spoke to Mr. Henry Draycott, Mr. Maurice Draycott and Mr. Frederick Daking, craftsmen working on the Cathedral, churchwardens, the Master of Music (Mr. W. M. Ross), assistant organist (Dr. Eric Leigh), oldest Cathedral songman, Mr. Walter Barnes, and Mr. R. Holmes (verger).

EMBROIDERY

The Cathedral embroideresses, headed by Mrs. M. Voisey, lined up behind some of their work, in which the Queen Mother expressed a great interest, and spoke to Miss A. Graham, Mrs. D. W. Shenton, Mrs. N. Plackett, Mrs. C. Fielding, and Mrs. M. Gillespie.

Towards the end of her visit to Derby, the Queen Mother spoke to many of the 30 ladies, most of whom act as Cathedral hostesses in preparing and serving teas and buffet meals to Cathedral visitors and guests.

The last presentation to her at the end of her five-hour packed tour of the town was Mr. T. Cooban, Chief Regional Officer at the Central Office of Information, Nottingham, who, with his team, was responsible for much of the organising of the Royal visit. She expressed to him how much she had enjoyed it, before leaving the Cathedral into Full Street, to more crowds.

Her car was waiting there to take her to Okeover Hall, home of Sir Ian Walker - Okeover, Lord Lieutenant of Derbyshire, and Lady Walker-Okeover, where she spent the night,

---

MAKING friends with Little John in the Market Place.

Not just cutting

DERBY CORPORATION'S Parks Department received Royal recognition yesterday.

During her tour, the Queen Mother paused in the Council House entrance to admire the beautiful flower arrangements, and asked for a geranium cutting.

Councillor L. L. Macdonald, chairman of the Parks Committee, offered her not a cutting, but a plant.

The plant was later transferred to one of the royal cars.

Their Graces sprint in

THE Duke and Duchess of Devonshire were a few minutes late arriving at Derby Council House for the official presentations and lunch. They dashed up the stairs, and joined the line of those being presented seconds before the Queen Mother was due to be introduced to them.

In official record

THIS was how the Queen Mother's visit to Derby was officially recorded in the Court Circular:

CLARENCE HOUSE, June 8

Queen Elizabeth the Queen Mother this morning visited the Royal Crown Derby works at Derby.

Her Majesty subsequently honoured the Mayor of Derby (Councillor J. J. Carty) with her presence at luncheon at the Council House.

This afternoon Queen Elizabeth the Queen Mother opened the restored Guildhall and later visited Derby Cathedral.

The Lady Jean Rankin, Capt. Alastair Aird and Capt. Ian Farquhar were in attendance.

Derbyshire talk for coffee club

Mr. Frank Pegg, speaking on Derbyshire to Normanton Ward Conservative Coffee Club, Derby, referred to its contrasting industries and the heritage of ingenuity and inventiveness of Derbyshire people.

Mr. W. N. K. Rowley expressed his appreciation for the hard work of members in the municipal election. He felt that a contributory factor in his defeat was the high proportion of floating voters which made up a considerable portion of Normanton Ward.

The *Evening Telegraph's* report of June 9, 1971 on the Queen Mother's delightfully informal visit.

Embroideresses from Derby Cathedral – headed by Mrs M. Voisey – lined up behind their work in which the Queen Mother expressed great interest.

The Queen Mother toured Derby Cathedral with the Bishop of Derby, the Rt Revd Cyril Bowles, the Provost, the Very Revd R.A. Beddoes, Archdeacon of Derby, the Venerable J.F. Richardson and Canon Paul Miller.

An informal walkabout in the Market Place for a smiling Queen Mother accompanied by the Mayor of Derby, Councillor Joe Carty in 1971.

After finishing her visit to the Guildhall, the Queen Mother tells Councillor Joe Carty, she is delighted that it has been restored.

Princess Alexandra chats with onlookers in Liversage Street before opening the new headquarters of Derby Borough Division of the British Red Cross Society on November 26, 1972.

In the regional Red Cross junior competition at Spondon School, the Princess had a sympathetic word for Mrs J. Hind who played the part of an injury "victim".

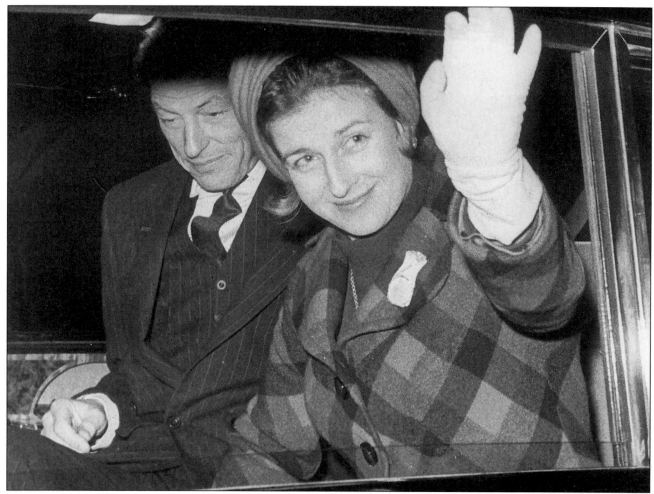

Angus Ogilvy came to Spondon School to meet his wife, and the two left together at the end of the Princess's visit.

Princess Margaret unveils the plaque at the Royal School for the Deaf on Ashbourne Road.

The Princess especially enjoyed her time with youngsters in the nursery at the Ashbourne Road School.

Teacher Miss P. Eccles shows art work by the children to the Princess.

Mr A. Ussher, Chief Caster at Royal Crown Derby – who had worked there since 1926 – shows Princess Anne how handles are placed on jugs in November 1974.

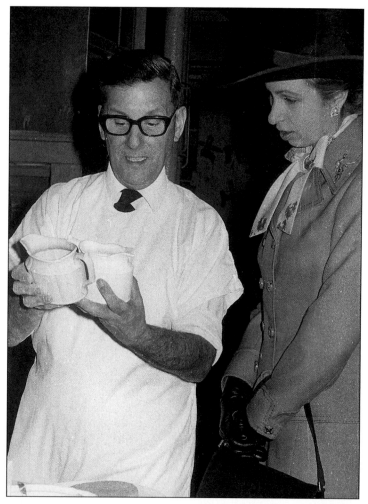

A welcome from the Mayor of Derby, Councillor George Salt, and the civic party, for Princess Anne in 1974.

Princess Alexandra learns some backstage secrets at Derby Playhouse in 1975.

Nurse Lyn Parkin presents a bouquet to the Princess at the Derbyshire Royal Infirmary.

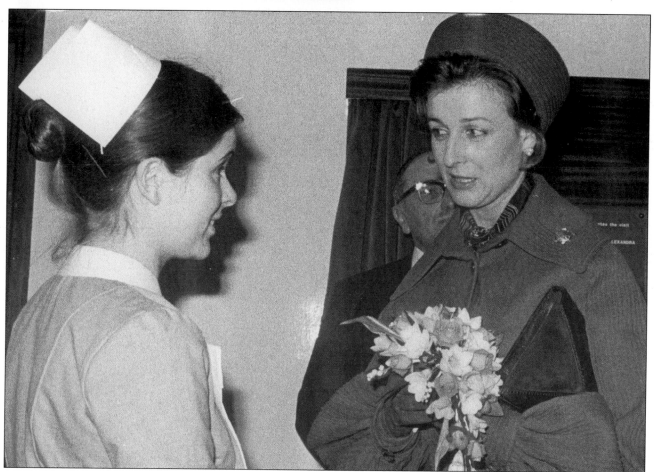

The Princess shares a laugh with Mrs Fanny Berry at the Derbyshire Royal Infirmary. Mrs Berry, then aged 105, could remember Queen Victoria's visit to Derby in 1891.

Jennifer Higginbottom, granddaughter of Councillor Les Shepley, chairman of the Leisure Services Committee, presented the Queen Mother with a posy of red roses at the Assembly Rooms on November 9, 1977.

The Queen Mother receives a Royal Crown Derby loving cup from the Mayor of Derby Jeffery Tillett when she visited Derby to open the Assembly Rooms in 1977. Weeks earlier she had graciously refused a far more costly gift because she felt it would be inappropriate to accept given the state of the economy.

The morning after the Assembly Rooms opening, the Queen Mother opened new buildings at St Christopher's Railway Home on Ashbourne Road.

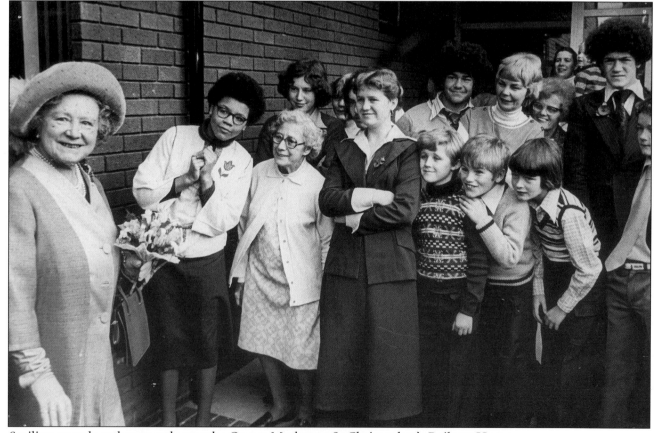

Smiling crowds gather to welcome the Queen Mother to St Christopher's Railway Home.

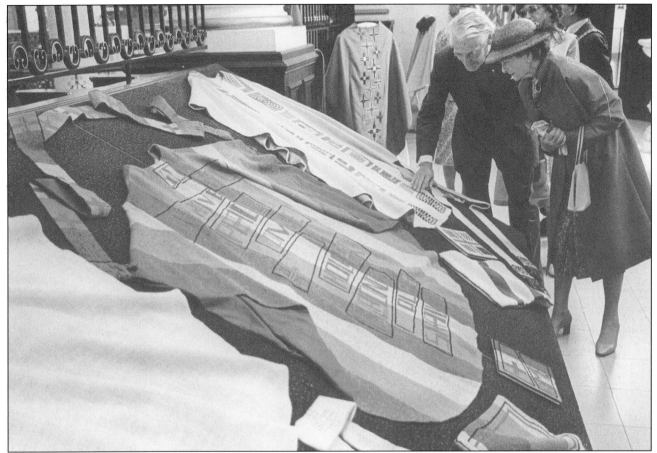

Princess Alice of Gloucester examines items on show as part of a national embroidery exhibition at Derby Cathedral in 1979. With her is the Provost of Derby, the Very Revd R. A. Beddoes.

Prince Charles delighted in the company of Mrs Fanny Berry at Warwick House old people's home, Bonsall Avenue, Littleover. She was due to celebrate her 109th birthday a week later.

A well-wisher presented Prince Charles with a Royal Crown Derby knife during his 1979 visit.

The Prince poses by the plaque marking Bonnie Prince Charlie's visit to Derby.

In front of the Bakewell Gates in Derby Cathedral, the Prince was presented with a cut glass goblet.

At Derbyshire's first Festival of Remembrance in the Assembly Rooms, Prince Charles met Boer War veteran Bill Williamson, aged 101, from Langley Mill who was with his daughter Mrs Grace Fowkes.

Princess Anne and her first husband, Captain Mark Philips, pictured at Locko Park where the Princess was competing in August 1978.

Chapter Six

The Honour of City Status

ON the day of the Queen's Silver Jubilee Celebration, Derby became a city. For a long time it had claimed the dubious honour of being the county's largest town; now it was the tenth town this century, the fourth since the end of World War Two to be elevated to city status.

Back in 1927 when All Saints' Church became Derby Cathedral, many thought that would be enough to qualify Derby as a city. But granting city status remained a prerogative of the Crown.

In the 1950s, there was evidence of wishful thinking when the hospital on Uttoxeter Road was called Derby City Hospital. During World War Two there was also a City of Derby Squadron in the RAF.

It was Derby Councillor Gerald Andrews who persevered in the 1970s in a fight to win city status for the town. The new Council of May 1976 was persuaded by him to make the latest of several applications for city status. Two months after the Jubilee Day announcement, the Queen came to Derby to personally deliver her Letters Patent, conferring on the borough the status of City with "all such rank, liberties, privileges and immunities as are incident to a city."

The Queen's schedule saw her arrive at Derby railway station at 10am on July 28, 1977.

Mayor of Derby, Councillor Jeffery Tillett received the Letters Patent from the Queen at the Council House and presented her with a Royal Crown Derby basket.

After a walkabout in Derby Market Place, the Queen left for Butterley Hall, where she carried out the official opening of Police Headquarters. The visit concluded with trips to Chesterfield and Mansfield. A Buckingham Palace official told an *Evening Telegraph* reporter that he had never seen so many flowers throughout the whole of the Queen's Jubilee tour as those that rained down in Derbyshire that day.

An estimated 60,000 people, sometimes ten-deep, lined the streets of Derby. More than 10,000 waited for a glimpse of the Queen and Prince Philip at Butterley.

The whole route – from Derby railway station to Chesterfield – was a sea of red, white and blue flags, bunting, streamers and home-made placards.

The area around Derby railway station was a noisy mass of colour from early morning. People tried for every possible vantage point – on the platform bridge, booking hall entrance, standing on station pillar stones and leaning out of windows and standing on top of buildings.

The crowd of several thousand got their first chance to cheer when the regimental band of the Worcestershire and Sherwood Foresters, led by its ram mascot, set off from the station on the processional route at 9.30am.

At exactly one minute before ten, the Royal train slid smoothly into platform one, where the Queen and the Duke were welcomed by Lord Lieutenant of Derbyshire, Sir Ian Walker-Okeover.

Waiting on platform one were selected senior British Rail employees and their wives and 18 Brownies from Nottingham.

As the Royal party left the station, the Queen, wearing a dress and coat of turquoise and white printed silk and Breton-shaped hat, was greeted by an enormous roar of approval and loyalty.

The first of the day's many unofficial floral gifts was given to her by young sisters Susanne, Michelle and Liza Jones of Baker Street, Alvaston.

As they handed over three posies the Queen asked them: "Have you picked these out of your garden?"

The children replied: "No, they are out of Nana's."

Punctually at 10.05am the Royal car pulled up at the main entrance of the Council House. The Royal party moved slowly up the steps, the Queen deep in conversation with Councillor Tillett, the Duke lingering to wave to the crowds.

A few minutes later the Royal couple appeared on the balcony to wave to the enthusiastic onlookers before returning to the steps for the presentation ceremony.

The serious note of the day was struck when the Queen handed over the Letters Patent. Then the couple left the steps to begin a Royal walkabout which won all hearts.

Mrs Mabel Hirst caught the eyes of the Queen first and handed over a posy on behalf of her pensioners' club. Then the flowers came thick and fast.

The Duke spent a lot of of his time joking and laughing with youngsters and on more than one occasion was left, grinning broadly, holding a bunch of flowers handed to him from the crowd.

Young children chanted: "We want the Queen" and the band of the 9th/12th Royal Lancers added to the carnival atmosphere.

As the walkabout was nearly at an end, the Royal progress was halted as a group of about 20 children surrounded the Queen.

The Queen changed her planned route from Derby to Butterley after receiving an invitation to call at The Leylands, Broadway, the Woollen Drapers' Cottage Homes of which she had become patron since her visit to the estate in 1957.

Lamp standards on the estate were decorated in red, white and blue metallic material and the elderly residents' cottages were festooned with bunting as the Queen drove slowly through from Broadway to Penny Long Lane where crowds of school children and residents assembled. The Royal car stopped briefly in the centre of the estate where the Queen was welcomed by Mr W.G. Eborn, chairman of the Cottage Homes.

Miss Hilda Boatman, 86, who had lived at the Leylands for 25 years, presented a bouquet. She was one of the residents who made a layette for Prince Andrew which the Queen accepted in 1960.

Over in Butterley the waiting crowds were kept entertained by live radio broadcasts covering the Royal visit in Derby which were played over PA equipment.

Arriving just seven minutes late, the Queen unveiled a commemorative wall plaque to officially open Derbyshire Police Headquarters.

The Bishop of Derby, the Right Revd Cyril Bowles dedicated the premises and the Royal couple then walked informally among the 10,000 people.

Again the Queen was surrounded by little ones and often threw back her head and laughed as, one after another, the presents came thick and fast.

But the award for the most dedicated Royal watchers that day probably goes to Mrs Lucy Taylor, of Havenbaulk Lane, Littleover, and Mrs Audrey Timmins, of Walnut Close, Chellaston, who had camped outside Derby Council House from 10pm the previous night to be sure of a good vantage point.

DERBY EVENING TELEGRAPH, Wednesday, July 27, 1977 I

Jubilee
CITY OF DERBY

A Derby Evening Telegraph special supplement to mark the Queen's Silver Jubilee grant of city status.

Elizabeth the Second by the Grace of God OF THE UNITED KINGDOM OF GREAT BRITAIN AND NORTHERN IRELAND AND OF OUR OTHER REALMS AND TERRITORIES QUEEN HEAD OF THE COMMONWEALTH DEFENDER OF THE FAITH To all to whom these Presents shall come Greeting Whereas We for divers good causes and considerations Us thereunto moving are graciously pleased to confer on the Borough of Derby the status of a City Now Therefore Know Ye that We of Our especial grace and favour & mere motion do by these Presents ordain declare and direct that the BOROUGH of DERBY shall henceforth have the status of a CITY and shall have all such rank liberties privileges and immunities as are incident to a City In Witness whereof We have caused these Our Letters to be made Patent Witness Ourself at Westminster the seventh day of June in the twenty-sixth year of Our Reign

BY WARRANT UNDER THE QUEEN'S SIGN MANUAL BOURNE

I AM delighted to have this opportunity to address a few words to the citizens of Derby, by way of foreword to this special supplement issued by the Derby Evening Telegraph. And may I begin by thanking and congratulating the newspaper on its initiative in producing this splendid issue? It will, I feel sure, be kept by thousands of its readers as a souvenir to be looked at again and again in the years to come by our citizens of the future as a record of this most important milestone in our city's history.

Many people ask me 'What does it mean — Derby's being a city? Does it really matter?'

I think the answer is in the one word — recognition. Just as we honour individuals for their achievements in the community whether in the fields of work, sport and entertainment, the arts, science and invention, politics, or the many facets of community work, national or international, so we can honour a whole community — and we do it by granting to it city status.

All these fields of endeavour that I have referred to are spheres in which Derby has through the ages been famed not only throughout the country but throughout the world: its industries whose names are international household words; its railway network; its football team; men of the calibre of Joseph Wright, Erasmus Darwin, Herbert Spencer, Henry Royce — the list is endless; and, at local level, such stalwarts as Samuel Plimsoll, Philip Noel-Baker, Arthur Sturgess,

What new status means to the Mayor

Henry Bemrose, Alec Ling — one could go on and on.

We have developed over the years an education service that is second to none. We have facilities for sports and recreation and the arts and parks and gardens, that are the envy of far larger cities.

Perhaps to the word recognition we might add the words appreciation and understanding: an appreciation of what has been done in the past to make Derby and all that the name Derby means what it is today; and an understanding — patient and caring — of what we are trying to do today to make Derby a better place to live in — to work in and to recreate ourselves in for the future.

This is what being a city means to me. I hope it is something that also touches the hearts of all those who are proud to call themselves its citizens.

The late President Kennedy once made the plea: do not ask what my country can do for me, but what can I do for it. In this simple thought is a whole philosophy, and it is a sentiment that every one of us might echo when we think of the city that bears the fair name of Derby.

Look at the coat of arms of our city. It bears the Latin inscription — Industria Virtus Fortitudo. Purists would no doubt translate this as Industry, Virtue and Fortitude. As we look ahead to the next twenty-five years of our life as the Queen's Jubilee City I should like to offer as a thought to each and every one of you this rather free translation of our city motto: Proud of our achievements of the past; Jealous of our fair reputation; and Determined to make our city a place worthy of its name.

Jeffery Tillett

Mayor of the City of Derby.

Front page of a special supplement printed by the *Derby Telegraph* on July 27, 1977.

A day when flowers cascaded down on the Royal couple began as soon as the couple arrived at Derby Station at 10am on July 28, 1977.

The Queen chats animatedly to the Mayor of Derby, Councillor Jeffery Tillett on the Royal couple's arrival at the Council House, while the Duke looks out at the waiting thousands of people with a smile.

A tumultuous roar greeted the appearance of the Royal couple on the balcony of the Council House, which the Queen had opened back in 1949.

Derby MP Walter Johnson is introduced to the Queen. Behind him is Derby's other MP, bearded Philip Whitehead.

Five-year-old Karen Peake of Breadsall presents a gift to the Queen as she leaves the Council House.

A relaxed moment with the Mayor of Derby after the presentation of the Letters Patent, which later went on show to the public. Also pictured are the Deputy Mayor, Councillor Eric Reid, and Mr Ernest Preston, City Secretary.

Royal aides help the Queen carry all her gifts from young admirers on the Market Place walkabout.

Union Flags were waved as youngsters clambered for a good view of Her Majesty. The lucky few came through the barriers to meet the Queen for a moment they never forgot.

Crowds were in place early in the morning for the Queen's arrival at Derby railway station.

The Queen, her arms full of flowers, prepares to receive more from eager children as she makes her progress through the Market Place on this most informal walkabout.

Residents of the Leyland Cottage Homes were delighted that the Queen made a detour from her planned route to see them – even though she only stopped long enough to collect a bouquet.

An unusual gift of a rag doll for the Queen at Butterley.

Smiling policewomen were laden with unofficial bouquets at Butterley.

Chapter Seven

Life is Sweet

AFTER the financial ups and downs of the 1970s, the 1980s saw life looking a lot sweeter. It was also the decade when the young Lady Diana Spencer began to win the hearts of the British people and change the style of the monarchy forever.

In Derby there were major visits by the Queen, Princess Margaret and Prince Charles.

The Queen found herself in the delightful situation of making a pre-Easter visit to Derbyshire confectioner Thorntons on March 15, 1985. As a sweet treat Her Majesty was given four specially decorated Easter Eggs bearing the names of her four grandchildren, Peter, Zara, William and Harry.

Swiss confisseur Walter Willen (55) iced the names in chocolate at Thorntons' £4-million factory at Swanwick.

The Queen watched rum truffles rolling off the production line. The sweets were later destroyed in keeping with strict hygiene rules because it had not been insisted that the Royal party wore overalls.

Earlier in the day, the Queen had visited Underhill, a housing scheme for the elderly in Two Dales, and Queen Elizabeth's Grammar School, Ashbourne.

After Swanwick, the Queen opened the £29-million Chesterfield and North Derbyshire Royal Hospital and visited Remploy at Whittington Moor.

In February 1981, Prince Charles turned his hand – and his feet – to all kinds of new pursuits during an eventful visit to the city. This scheduled five-hour visit lasted well over six, and he skipped his lunch hour to cram as much as he could into the day.

It was just a few days after his engagement to Lady Diana Spencer, and Charles promised the residents who gave gifts and cards that she would be with him on his next visit.

Arriving by train at Derby, the Prince was met by the Lord Lieutenant of Derbyshire, Colonel Peter Hilton, and made his first stop the Guru Arjan Dev Sikh Temple in Shaftesbury Street.

In keeping with tradition he took off his shoes, covered his head – with a large white handkerchief – and sat on the floor surrounded by Sikh temple officials.

At the Madeley Centre he joined in some spirited disco dancing and at the Ukrainian Club in Charnwood Street he joined in with the traditional folk dancing of a very different style. Afterwards, looking flushed but not out of breath, he commented: "It takes we young ones to show them how to do it."

At the Dom Polski down the road, he also waved away a glass of orange juice or sherry in favour of a glass of Polish Vodka which he downed in one before following the traditional custom of slinging the empty glass over his shoulder where it smashed to pieces on the floor.

More seriously, the Prince paid tribute to the Polish airman, telling the members of Dom Polski: "You fought so bravely and made so many sacrifices in the war that we'll never forget what you did."

At the Drop-in Coffee Bar in Pear Tree, the Prince showed his skill at table football and pool. He also visited Hardwick Girls' school and the Sikh Temple on St James's Road.

At the Serbian Orthodox Church, Lower Dale Road, the Prince was presented with a Chuturica – an engraved hand-made flask designed to carry the Serbian national drink Sljivovica, a form of plum brandy. It was hung around the Prince's neck on a wide ribbon by the Church President Mr Rad Andjelic.

"Now I know what it feels like to be a Saint Bernard dog," joked Prince Charles.

Two small children broke away from the police cordon when the Prince reached the Normanton Road Serbian Orthodox Church to present him with bunches of yellow freesias.

The Very Revd Abbot Seraphimde Scouratov presented the Prince with the traditional Serbian welcome of bread and salt.

The Prince ended his day in Burton upon Trent.

Throughout the 1980s, Prince Charles avidly followed his beloved country pursuits whenever time allowed, with the media usually not far behind. In November 1984, for instance, he was snapped by the *Evening Telegraph* as he joined the South Notts Hunt at Idridgehay, near Wirksworth.

On June 29, 1988, the Prince headed a glittering guest list at Kedleston Hall in his role as patron of the Kedleston Hall appeal which was bidding to raise £2-million to keep the Hall open and pay its running costs.

The Derbyshire house was designed by Robert Adam in the 1700s and because of the Prince's interest in architecture he was delighted to take a special interest in the building.

In 1984, Princess Margaret was in Derby to promote the children's charity the NSPCC. At a service in Derby Cathedral, she personally thanked many youngsters as they handed over donations totalling £45,000 for the Derbyshire NSPCC appeal.

Wearing a fur-trimmed Cossack-style hat and royal blue cape over a patchwork design dress, the Princess walked to the Cathedral through a guard of honour of ex-servicemen and women.

She received more than 400 purses containing NSPCC donations during the one and a quarter hour service. Next stop was the Assembly Rooms, where the Princess met more children and signed the visitors' book.

Later, at the YMCA on London Road, the Princess unveiled a plaque on new living quarters. She spoke to one resident, 17-year-old Andrew Devine about his room and his job prospects.

"She was very nice and very easy to talk to," said Andrew.

As a parting gift, Princess Margaret was presented with a Royal Crown Derby loving cup by the Mayor of Derby, Councillor Ron Longdon.

After a few visits to the county, the Princess of Wales made her first major visit to the city in February 1985.

Freezing temperatures failed to spoil the day which saw Diana visit the Normanton Road annex of Derby College of Further Education. After lunch the Princess was driven to Gosforth Road to visit the Wetherby Day Centre, where more than 180 people with disabilities demonstrated their working and artistic skills.

Just down the road, at the Community Task Force Unit, the Princess joked: "I'll never get home in time to make the tea".

One onlooker, little Hayley Repton, aged three, of Jubalton Close, Alvaston earned the Princess's heartfelt sympathy when she confessed: "I'm cold and I've been crying a bit."

Princess Diana replied: "I'm sorry, I suppose I have been talking too long".

Then she dashed back to East Midlands International Airport where Prince Charles arrived to fly her home.

In 1987, Princess Diana was back in Derby to visit Royal Crown Derby on Osmaston Road. The Princess signed "Diana" on the base of a commemorative candlestick at the factory. A wise-cracking photographer asked her if she had spelt it correctly.

"I make the jokes round here," warned the Princess to shrieks of laughter.

Earlier, the Princess in a bright blue coat, Russian hat and black boots, had visited the £7.5-million Ilkeston Community Hospital on Heanor Road.

Yet again the visit took place in freezing weather, on December 10, and a group of youngsters from Ivy House school had to be warmed up in a police van with hot drinks after they endured a long wait for the Princess outside Royal Crown Derby.

But the Princess made their wait worthwhile when she stopped and accepted a posy from pupil Shabmim Mushtaq, aged five.

The Duke of Edinburgh on a flying visit to Rolls-Royce in November 1981.

Princess Anne's love of show jumping led her to make several visits to the Derby area. Here she is competing at Locko Park Horse Trials in August 1980.

Princess Anne's first husband, Captain Mark Philips at Locko, again in 1980.

Princess Anne received a gift from Mrs Nora Nicholson during a visit to Locko Hall in October 1980. Looking on is Lady Winifred Hilton, wife of the then Lord Lieutenant of Derbyshire, Colonel Peter Hilton.

Four-year-old Lara Scott of Allestree presented a posy to Princess Anne when she visited members of the St John Ambulance at Carrington Street on July 27, 1982.

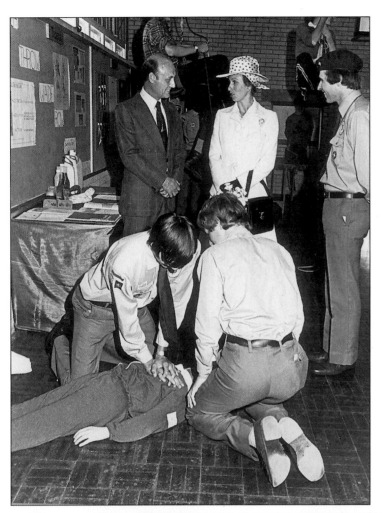

The 73rd Allestree Scout Group give a life saving demonstration during the Princess's 1982 visit.

The Prince, turbaned with a handkerchief and garlanded, joins his hosts in prayer at the Sikh Temple, Shaftesbury Street.

Elaine McKellar joined the Prince in a game of table football at the Drop-in Coffee Bar in Pear Tree.

Delighted youngsters in traditional costume at the Polish Club, Charnwood Street, were thrilled to meet the heir to the throne.

The Prince quickly accepted an invitation to boogie on down with youngsters at the Madeley Centre's Disco Club.

"It takes we young ones to show them how to do it," said the Prince after joining in with some spirited dancing with the Ukrainian Dance Assembly on Charnwood Street.

"Don't waste all your film on me," chided the Prince when the *Evening Telegraph* snapped him out with the South Notts Hunt near Idridgehay in November 1984.

Princess Margaret unveils a plaque to open the YMCA extension in December 1984.

A posy of orchids for the Princess as she meets officials at the YMCA.

A Royal Crown Derby Loving Cup is presented to Princess Margaret to commemorate her December 1984 visit by the Mayor of Derby, Councillor Ron Longdon. Only two others existed at the time and both had been presented to the Queen Mother on previous visits to Derby.

It was a big day for eight-year-old Claire Longdon, granddaughter of the Mayor of Derby, Councillor Ron Longdon, who presented a posy to Princess Diana on Tuesday February 20, 1985, when the Princess arrived at the Derby College of Further Education annex, Normanton Road. The Princess was so concerned about the freezing temperatures that she bustled young Claire indoors out of the cold.

The Princess took a great interest in the work of students at the Normanton Road annex of Derby College of Further Education.

More than 180 people with disabilities showed their work to the Princess at Wetherby Industrial Unit, Ascot Drive.

At the Community Task Force Centre, Ascot Drive, the Princess surprised trainee builder Wayne Morris, of the Mackworth Estate, who was putting the finishing touches to a chimney stack – at floor level. She strode across to shake his hand and noticed his tattooed hand and asked him all about it.

An enthusiastic Royal fan gets a close-up shot for her photo album.

Community Task Force trainee Mark Murphy stops work on a fireplace as the Princess and unit manager Mr J. Linthwaite clear up a few points.

Craig Griffiths, a multi-skills student on a YTS scheme at the Derby College of Further Education, Normanton Road annex, shows the Princess how to fix together a pair of nesting boxes, inscribed William and Harry on brass plates – a gift for the Princess's sons from the students.

Waiting crowds make the most of a Royal walkabout during Princess Diana's visit.

Walter Willen poses with the four eggs he decorated for the Queen's grandchildren when she visited Thorntons at Swanwick in March 1985.

A four-foot high chocolate bunny took Thorntons Swiss confisseur Walter Willen and his team two weeks to make using 24 coats of chocolate. It was destined for the nearby Alfreton Park Wood school. Also pictured with the Queen and Mr Willen is Thorntons managing director Mr John Thornton.

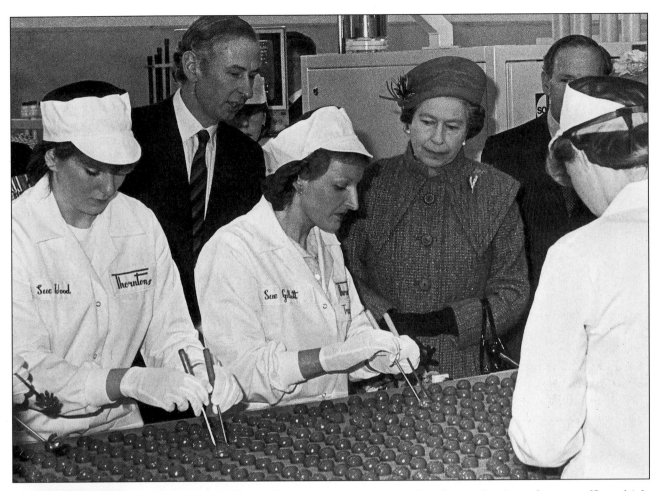

The Queen watches the production of rum truffles which were later destroyed because of the decision not to ask the Royal party to wear hygiene overalls.

Princess Diana arrives at East Midlands Airport on Thursday December 10, 1987. Behind her is the Lord Lieutenant of Derbyshire, Colonel Peter Hilton.

A china plaque marks the Princess's visit to open a new section of Royal Crown Derby.

Crown Derby worker Glenis Burrows discusses her work with the Princess.

Mayor of Derby, Councillor Mrs Nancy Wawman hands over badger and rabbit paperweights for the Princes William and Harry and two fluffy frogs "for them to throw around at Christmas".

Prince Charles gazes thoughtfully at the stunning architecture of Kedleston Hall when he headed the glittering guest list at a by-invitation-only benefit in July 1988.

Kedleston Hall – Prince Charles leads out other guests as they raise money to maintain the historic building.

Chapter Eight

The People's Princess

I N the early 1990's, Princess Diana continued to monopolise media attention. Her two visits to the Derby area in this period saw scenes of adulation unparalleled in the county.

The *Evening Telegraph's* edition of Wednesday September 9, 1992, dubbed her "The People's Princess" – a title which stayed with her for the rest of her life. To many it is how she will always be remembered.

On that day, Diana visited Borrowash's Birkin lace factory. She had flown into East Midlands Airport with Prince Charles. Together they called at the Queen's Medical Centre in Nottingham where he had been treated for a twisted knee the previous Saturday.

While the Prince continued a tour of duties in Nottingham, the Princess became the fifth member of the House of Windsor to visit the Birkin company.

King George V and Queen Mary had toured the company's Nottingham plant in 1914 and Queen Elizabeth II was a visitor in 1953. The Princess Royal, Princess Anne, had visited the Borrowash factory in 1986.

Civic dignitaries lined up to meet the Princess of Wales. But once the formalities were over, Diana made straight for hundreds of flag-waving school children.

The youngsters from Redhill Primary, Ockbrook, Ashbrook Infant and Junior and Draycott Primary clamoured to give the Princess posies. Birkin's assistant managing director, Barry Stocks, guided the Princess around the factory and explained the lace-making process.

He said afterwards: "The Princess of Wales does a fantastic job for the British textile and fashion industries and we are delighted she could come."

Wearing a smart two-piece Royal blue suit, the Princess delighted fans with an impromptu walkabout. Dorothy Darlington of Kirlees Avenue, Spondon, travelled to Borrowash with her four sisters for the chance to see Diana.

She said: "She was absolutely gorgeous. We want her back in Derbyshire. She has made Borrowash special."

Earlier that year, in April, the Princess brought a ray of sunshine to Amber Valley during a series of engagements in Riddings and Belper.

Wearing a green fitted suit and a pink top, she opened Riddings Park Community Centre and, visited Whitemoor Day Centre for the disabled on John O'Gaunt's Way. Police security was extra vigilant following a terrorist shooting in Derby city centre.

At Babington Hospital, the Princess met patients and staff and opened a Red Cross Centre in the grounds.

A planned helicopter arrival in Derby by Diana's sister-in-law, the Duchess of York on Valentine's Day 1991, was thwarted by fog. A last minute change of plan saw her dash to Derby by train – an hour behind schedule.

But she still said she was delighted with what she called "the best welcome I have had for ages."

In a red jacket and black skirt, the Duchess also sported a gold heart-shaped badge for the Royal Variety Club of Britain's Heart Beat appeal.

On her first stop, hundreds of cheering school children from six primary schools packed the driveway of Sinfin Community School.

A colourful Chinese dragon greeted the Duchess in a display to celebrate the Chinese New Year.

At the Oast House Hotel, Foresters Park, the Duchess helped launch the Derbyshire Royal National Institute for the Blind's £175,000 Looking Glass Appeal.

It was then off to Derbyshire Children's Hospital to chat to staff and patients before unveiling a plaque to mark her visit.

The Duchess also called at the Access Centre in London Road where estranged parents can meet their children on neutral ground. A busy day ended with the official opening of the refurbished Joseph Wright Gallery in Derby Museum.

In 1994 the Duchess returned to the City prompted by a letter from deaf student, Asif Iqbal, aged 18. He asked her to visit him, so the Duchess agreed to pop in and see him at the Royal School for the Deaf on Ashbourne Road, which was celebrating its centenary year.

Asif said: "When I got the letter I could not believe it. I am very happy she is coming and I can't wait to see her. I know she has a lot of interest in deaf people and I think she is learning sign language."

The Duchess's project manager Christine

Gallaher explained: "She reads all her letters and this one just stood out. It was such a sweet note that she said she would really like to meet him and his friends at the school."

The Duchess made a two-hour private visit to the school on March 22. She proved she did know some sign language and also spoke through an interpreter.

Two more major visits by the Queen were the focus of intense interest.

In May 1992 the Queen carried out a gruelling schedule, officially opening Carsington Reservoir, visiting Matlock, Wirksworth, Alton Manor and Derby.

In the city Her Majesty visited the Derbyshire Royal Infirmary and met consultants who treated victims of the Kegworth air crash. She also opened the newly-refurbished Queen's Leisure Centre.

The Lord Lieutenant of Derbyshire, Colonel Peter Hilton, said it was "the best Royal visit we have ever had and the Queen enjoyed herself tremendously because of the warmth of Derbyshire people."

At the DRI, the Queen met three youngsters in the Accident and Emergency unit and also chatted with three women who were receiving treatment at the hospital's pioneering hand surgery unit. She then officially opened the Guy Pulvertaft Hand Centre.

Consultant Paul Pritty said the Queen asked about the injuries of passengers involved in the Kegworth air crash and told him she had met one of the victims on a previous Royal visit.

The Queen also took a step back in time when she saw an exhibition to mark the centenary of the hospital.

At the Queen's Leisure Centre, the Queen was presented with a print of a painting depicting her great great grandmother, Queen Victoria's visit to Derby in 1891.

In 1997, the Queen and her husband returned to open Derby County's Pride Park Stadium. The Queen, alone, visited the Royal School for the Deaf and the Derbyshire Children's Hospital while the Duke of Edinburgh visited Rolls-Royce.

After the Queen joined him at Rolls-Royce for lunch the couple left for engagements at Hardwick Hall and in Bolsover.

The Royal couple arrived by train and went straight to Pride Park where a crowd of 30,000 awaited them. The Queen was introduced to Derby County players and officials, and she and the Duke toured the ground standing in an open-topped vehicle to acknowledge the cheering throng.

On Ashbourne Road, local people had climbed on to rooftops to catch a glimpse of the Queen arriving at the Royal School for the Deaf.

She saw youngsters in the main hall "sing" the hymn *God Is With Us* and *God Save the Queen* in sign language before watching part of a circus life production put on by youngsters. The Queen presented two awards to outstanding pupils Ashley Kitchen, aged 11, and Samantha Brentnall, aged 15.

The Queen also saw the school's pioneering £800,000 sign language video centre where videos of books were being produced in sign language.

More than 300 children from Wren Park Primary School, Mickleover, greeted the Queen at the Derbyshire Children's Hospital. During her tour the Queen visited the Ronnie MacKeith Centre, the physiotherapy department, the intensive care unit and two wards.

Patient Dale Handley gave the Queen a drawing of a kite which he had done, and Littleover Women's Institute members Jenny Outram and Julia Sim gave the Queen a quilted and embroidered collage.

Meanwhile, at Rolls-Royce, the Duke took control of an engine throttle and revved up a £10-million Trent 800 while touring the R-R Test Control Room at Wilmore Road.

The Duke's 90-minute visit saw him arrive at the New Engine Assembly and Test building where he unveiled a commemorative plaque. As on his previous visits to the company, Prince Philip strayed from his official timetable to chat with employees about their work.

At 12.15pm the Duke joined the Queen for lunch in the Sir Henry Royce Centre.

The Duchess of York exchanged banter with photographers at Sinfin Community School on Valentine's Day 1991.

Not one to stand on ceremony, the Duchess leaps on to a bench to get a better look at the hundreds of children cheering her at Sinfin Community School.

Cheering youngsters welcome the smiling Duchess in 1991.

The Duchess visited Derby in 1991 to launch Derbyshire Royal National Institute for the Blind's £175,000 Looking Glass Appeal. Here, she watches Philip Yates type in Braille.

Four-year-old Natasha Taylor made an impromptu presentation of a bunch of tulips to the Duchess when she visited the Access Centre in Queen's Hall, London Road.

Meeting Princess Diana was just too much for Tom Birch, aged three, who burst into tears as he and his mother handed over some flowers during a walkabout in King Street, Belper, on Tuesday April 28, 1992.

Rachel Knowles presents a colourful posy of freesias to the Princess at Belper's Whitemoor Day Centre.

Derbyshire Red Cross President Margaret Henry shares a laugh with the Princess in the grounds of Babington Hospital.

Lilly Tonks, aged 77, hands over a posy to the Princess of Wales during her Belper walkabout.

A laughing Princess joins in a game of scrabble with staff and patients at Babington Hospital, Belper.

A touching moment as Diana takes the hands of an elderly patient at Babington Hospital.

Junior Red Cross member Carly Allen, 13, has a chat about baby care as she shows the Princess a demonstration doll at the new British Red Cross meeting room at Belper.

Cheering youngsters wait for the Queen during her May 1992 visit.

The Queen, in a purple floral dress and hat, laughed with staff at the Derbyshire Royal Infirmary who were dressed up to mark the hospital's centenary.

Laura Parkin, aged five, of Littleover, watched by her great-uncle, the Mayor of Derby, Councillor John Keith, presents a bouquet to the Queen outside the Queen's Leisure Centre. The bouquet was identical to one presented to Queen Victoria on her visit to Derby 101 years before.

Pamela Storer of the Derbyshire St John Ambulance Princess Anne Training Centre in Trinity Street shared a joke with the Queen before presenting her with a first-aid kit.

Patriotic Colin Edwards swopped headgear with Mayor John Keith as he waited for the Queen outside the Queen's Leisure Centre. He later presented Her Majesty with an album of Royal photographs.

A thoughtful moment for the Princess during her Borrowash visit.

Evening BORROWASH
Telegraph

WEDNESDAY, SEPTEMBER 9, 1992   No. 34,616   25p   VOICE OF DERBY

A RIGHT
ROYAL
WELCOME

● Hundreds of schoolchildren, including pupils from Redhill Primary School, Ockbrook, turned out in force to welcome The Princess of Wales during her visit to Borrowash this afternoon.

THE PEOPLE'S PRINCESS

VILLAGERS turned out today to give the people's most popular Royal a heart-warming welcome to Derbyshire.

The Princess of Wales visited Borrowash's Birkin lace factory this afternoon.

Dressed in a radiant Royal blue two-piece, she met workers, schoolchildren and, at the end of her visit, went on an impromptu walk-about.

Earlier she had flown into East Midlands International Airport accompanied by Prince Charles, who went on to visit the Queen's Medical Centre in Nottingham where he was treated for twisted knee on Saturday.

▶ **MORE COLOUR PICTURES IN TOMORROW'S TELEGRAPH**

The Borrowash edition of the *Derby Telegraph* marked the Princess of Wales visit on Wednesday September 9, 1992.

Listening carefully to youngsters from local schools, the Princess outside the Birkin Group at Borrowash.

Union Flags flutter in the breeze as the Princess walks about in Borrowash.

More gifts of flowers for the People's Princess.

The Duchess of York is welcomed to the Royal School for the Deaf in 1994. She flew in by helicopter on a two-hour private visit after student Asif Iqbal wrote to invite her.

Showing her knowledge of sign language, the Duchess at the Royal School for the Deaf.

The Duchess brought laughter and joy on her visit to Derby in 1994.

Signing the visitors book at the Royal School for the Deaf.

The Queen arrives at Pride Park Stadium with Derby County chairman Lionel Pickering.

The Queen unveils the plaque at Pride Park on July 18, 1997.

An open-top car takes the Queen, the Duke, Mr Pickering and Derby County manager Jim Smith round the pitch to wave at 30,000 fans.

Rams players (left to right) Robbie van der Laan, Ron Willems and Christian Dailly – two Dutchman and a Scot – are introduced to the Queen.

Deaf students perform God Save the Queen in sign language in the main hall of the Royal School for the Deaf.

Seven-year-old Rachel Severn presents a posy to the Queen.

Ashley Kitchen, aged 11, receives a cup from the Queen to mark his outstanding performance at the Royal School for the Deaf. Buckingham Palace requested and used this photograph on its own Internet Website for several months as an example of the Queen's duties.

At the Royal School for the Deaf's video suite the Queen watched a video about herself which had had sign language added. Here she shares a joke with the school's Colin Ashmore and Sir Richard Morris.

The Queen with a young patient at the Derbyshire Children's Hospital in Uttoxeter New Road, Mickleover.

The Queen leaves Rolls-Royce and says her farewell to the Mayor of Derby, Councillor John Fuller and the High Sheriff of Derbyshire, Richard Perkins.

All the photographs in this book can be ordered as black and white prints. The visits of the 1990s in Chapter Eight are available in colour. Telephone the Derby Evening Telegraph Photographic Department on 01332 291111 Ext 3803 for more details.